# DISRUPTING
# SACRED
# COWS

# DISRUPTING SACRED COWS

## NAVIGATING & PROFITING IN THE NEW ECONOMY

**GARRETT GUNDERSON**

WITH **COREY WERT**

**MEDIA**

Published 2022 by Gildan Media LLC
aka G&D Media
www.GandDmedia.com

Front cover design by Tom McKeveny

Interior design by Chinook Design, Inc. (chinoooktype.com)

Library of Congress Cataloging-in-Publication Data is available upon request

ISBN: 978-1-7225-0568-4

10 9 8 7 6 5 4 3 2 1

# CONTENTS

**To the Producers:**

*The world is changing rapidly. This book is for those who seek knowledge over ignorance, truth over deception, freedom over security, and responsibility over captivity. A time of disruption is at hand, a time to displace antiquated philosophies and myths and instead live a life of abundance, prosperity, and value. Will you answer the call?*

# A Gift

MAY I GIVE YOU A GIFT? HOW ABOUT THREE?
Because you're reading *Disrupting Sacred Cows,* I'd like to give you two complimentary companion books. The first is my *New York Times* bestseller, *Killing Sacred Cows* (the prelude to this book). The second is the important follow-up, *What Would Billionaires Do?*

*Killing Sacred Cows* challenged convention and pulled back the curtain to reveal the old financial paradigms and models that were positioned as helpful but were in fact destructive to wealth accumulation. More than ten years later, the myths and models I challenged in the book have begun deteriorating at an accelerated rate. The book is your guide to identifying those myths, and your roadmap around the financial pitfalls that reduce wealth. With finance, and the world, becoming increasingly difficult to navigate, *Killing Sacred Cows* is even more relevant now than when it was first released.

*What Would Billionaires Do?* gives you my tactics and methods for securing cash, capturing wealth, and creating a legacy. It illustrates a strategy I started using when I was nineteen years old and that continues to serve me to this day. The book then takes it one step further by expanding on the ideas and philosophies that some of the wealthiest families have used (both correctly and incorrectly) to build a legacy that lasts.

As a final gift, Wealth Factory, a firm that focuses on supporting people to get their financial houses in order, plug financial leaks, and identify the financial professionals required for the implementation of the strategies you will learn about in this book, will also provide a complimentary one-on-one support call to determine your financial strengths and highlight the best path for you to reach economic independence in ten years or less.

Go to WealthFactory.com/disrupting to claim your gifts.

# Introduction

M ORE THAN TEN YEARS AFTER I WROTE MY FIRST BOOK, the *Wall Street Journal* #1 bestseller *Killing Sacred Cows,* its philosophy is more relevant than ever. Our world has changed immensely over the last decade, however, and it is essential to take a fresh look at these concepts and see how they can help us navigate the next few years. We are witnessing the greatest wealth transfer in history, and it is only getting faster with the massive disruption due to blockchain, hyper-inflation, and the displacement of the old rules of investing.

This book is not an update to *Killing Sacred Cows.* It's a sequel.

Since I pointed out the destructive mythology around building wealth, Wall Street, and retirement planning in that book, the wealth gap has widened, the value of money has been decimated, and even the literal notion of money has been redefined. It has become more digital, more confusing, and less personal, and the consequences of inflation are imminent.

Accepting the dangerous dogma of these myths that undermine and destroy prosperity has swift and severe results. Without proper principles to guide them, people chase returns that require unnecessary risk and speculation that leads to loss. Or they buy into sophisticated stories about investments peddled by salesmen that amount to little more than gambling.

"Invest early, often, and always" is a mantra that will lead to disappointment and destruction. Blue chip companies that were a sure thing in the past will eventually be replaced by blockchain or other emerging technologies, even AI (artificial intelligence).

We are living in a new world, one where anyone can succeed—*if* they know the rules and don't get played by them, that is. Strategies that were once accessible only to Wall Street moguls and used in secret backroom deals are now being democratized. Thanks to crowdfunding, online communities, and strategic partnerships, opportunities that used to require millions of dollars and the right connections are now readily available to anyone looking to start a business, all with minimal to no up-front investment.

This is not a time to rely on gurus who are great at selling advice rather than making their money by following it. In an age when anyone can become a "thought leader" with just a few videos, Instagram posts, or a long article that gets turned into a book, their "free advice" can ultimately cost you more than ever.

With billions upon billions of dollars dumped into marketing, the message has become, "Hey, we're smart, just trust us." Most financial gurus make money very differently from the way they tell you to make it. When they say, "It takes money to make money," they mean it takes *your* money for them to make money. When they say, "High risk equals high return," sure, you take the risk, they get the return. This is a win/lose proposition that only stops when you stop letting money intimidate you.

And it's not just you allowing money to feel complex, it is a deliberate message from Wall Street, financial institutions, banks, and retirement planners that says you can't be trusted to make these choices, you don't have the time, and you should really just rely on them since they are so much smarter than everyone else.

Most people relate money to spreadsheets and numbers, which supports the complexity narrative and is one of the major reasons why most people feel they will never truly understand money.

In this book, I shed light on the scarcity mindset that holds people captive to a life of financial struggle and frustration. I simplify money, illustrate how to focus your time where it matters most in your finances, and teach you how to deal with the destructive, ingrained childhood beliefs that created the habits and beliefs holding you back from taking responsibility for your money.

Once you understand what money is, how others make it, and your own unique Investor DNA, you can become a better investor, cut out the noise, save time, and take responsibility for your investments, financial foundation, and the outcome of your income.

At times, this book will take the concepts from *Killing Sacred Cows* and apply them to today's world and economy. There is no requirement to read the previous book in order to benefit from this one and understand what to do now; but as a gift, a download of *Killing Sacred Cows* is included and can be downloaded at WealthFactory.com/disrupting. The download of *Killing Sacred Cows* provides additional case studies, statistics, comparisons, summaries, and visuals. In this book, the focus is on diving deeper into the causes of scarcity and how to address and minimize them. Rather than show you graphs and charts, I share practical ways for you to improve your finances today.

Now, before we get started, it is important to understand that I did not come from money. My family never really understood money. In fact, they feared it. They believed there would never be enough, and that whatever they had could be confiscated at any moment. This led to stress and scarcity, creating a self-imposed mindset of personal poverty.

The scarcity mindset impacts marriages, causes fights, and can even destroy families. It's like an unseen virus, infecting a computer; it slows processing speeds and holds up progress. And it puts your prosperity and financial freedom at risk. I've witnessed and experienced this personally, watching my grandfather lose his entire relationship with his sister over money.

But I've also seen positive transformations over the years. Not just in my own life, but also in the lives of my parents and my readers. That's what ignites my passion for teaching, supporting, and empowering, not transacting. My purpose is to bring a perspective that simplifies, addresses, and removes the underlying issues, thereby allowing for more prosperity.

It is also important to note, I **do not** invest people's money. I **am not** selling any financial products or representing any financial institutions. I even sold my consulting firm, Wealth Factory, in 2021.

I saw the limitations and consequences of retirement planning first-hand when I sold mutual funds from 1998–2000 and life insurance from 1998–2005. This was profitable, but I also found it unfulfilling. To be candid: there was no way to discover and call out financial myths when my paycheck came primarily from the system I have worked for years to expose.

This book isn't about taking on risk and spending your days chasing returns. It is about creating a life you don't want to retire from and enjoying a better quality of life along the way.

The key is to build a solid financial foundation so you will have more clarity, confidence, and peace of mind. Rather than just handing money to long-term retirement plans and hoping for the best, or blindly trusting Wall Street, you will discover ways to heal your relationship with money and learn how to invest in your greatest asset: yourself.

So, how do we start? Well, this process begins with awareness, and identifying any strategies (or lack thereof) that are not creating value for you now or are unlikely to do so in the future. By uncovering the beliefs, models, and myths that undermine wealth creation, you will be able to define your own personal Investor DNA. With this newfound awareness, you'll be equipped to simplify and reduce risk while becoming a better investor in the process.

Part one of this book explains the deeper components and under-pinnings of money and wealth. Guiding questions will assist you as you uncover the subtle lies you believe about money, and the heavy consequences that believing those lies can bring. Uncovering and removing the underpinnings of scarcity while creating your vision from a place of abundance is the foundational philosophical construct required for lasting wealth and quality of life.

Part two contains a mix of the key philosophies from *Killing Sacred Cows,* updated for today's economy, and combines these philosophies with very practical financial strategies and techniques (something missing from *Killing Sacred Cows*) that lead to immediate improvements in cash flow.

Financial independence begins with you. Take care of yourself, build a foundation, and understand the fundamentals. It is imperative that you handle your life before sacrificing for your community or the world. If you skip this step, which many will say is selfish, you may get caught in a trap that leads to exhaustion and risk. It is great to want to help others and give to charity, but if you don't handle your basics first, the resulting stress will inhibit your ability to add value or think clearly, ultimately robbing you of precious time by inviting worry.

When you trade time for money—when your time is no longer your own—your ability to give is diminished by stress. If you have bills to pay, obligations to meet, and people to please (at your own expense), you lose energy, creativity, and the ability to deliver your best.

The government and corporations are not coming to save you. It is time to take responsibility for yourself. You don't have to do this by your-self, but you must be responsible for your money, your words, and your actions, for your life and its lessons. No matter where you are or what you have done, remember: we are all perfectly imperfect. It is your time to learn your own lessons and live a fulfilled life.

# Chapter One

# Listen to Your Inner Voice

THIS, OF COURSE, IS NOT A BOOK ABOUT ACTUAL COWS. A "sacred cow" is an unquestioned belief, often a long-standing tradition, that is handed down to us and likely causes us to base our happiness or success on something that is out of our control. The myth is that if we just sacrifice, work hard, trade our time for money, and hand over 10% of our earnings to investments (that we barely understand), we will have enough—someday. However, that someday never seems to be today. Believing life will be good eventually is a trap, a sacred cow that absolutely must be disrupted.

By holding on to these sacred cows, we're living in the past, making choices based upon historical circumstances or what someone else decided. Maybe someone in your family lost their home during the Great Depression, and family stories have been passed down through the generations about how to avoid this outcome. Maybe at one point a grandmother had a small oven, so she cut off the sides of the ham to fit, and the family is still cutting off the sides of the ham even though ovens are much bigger now.

Or maybe you believe you're just not valuable enough, or lovable enough, so you're hustling and working hard, hoping that someday you will have enough, feel like enough, or earn enough to overcome the uncertainty, insecurity, and doubt created by childhood trauma and pain. Society promotes the idea that success is measured by money or the amount of stuff we have. This leads people to chase riches in the hope that material wealth will make them feel better or more appreciated. This is because they don't understand that life's real value and wealth come from within.

> **Value**
>
> *Anything of worth that, when provided to another, creates utility or joy for both parties. Value can come in many forms, such as physical gifts, kind words, and acts of service. Wealth is created when value is exchanged.*

Why do we buy into these sacred cows? Because they are reinforced throughout society by ads, articles, award shows, movies, etc. Making more money as the primary focus of having a better life is planted in our culture. But how much money, and how happy will it make us? There are elements of truth to the argument that more money creates a better life, but there is so much more to the story. It is the subtle lies around money that hold us captive. The obvious lies are easier to notice and avoid, but the subtle ones are harder to detect.

These lies form the myths that destroy the possibility of prosperity in both our personal lives and our finances. On a personal level, they are undermining beliefs such as *Who am I to do this?* or *I'm not good enough* or *Nobody's been able to do that before, so why would/could/should I?* These lies are what hold us in place and keep us from moving, trying, and growing.

Most of these sacred cows are reinforced by a lack of responsibility: we believe that wealth or "the good life" happen by luck or chance, or are predetermined by the family we were born into or by our innate capabilities, and that we can't change ourselves or our circumstances.

One of the more impactful lies perpetuated upon the masses is the notion that happiness exists outside of ourselves or in the stuff we have. This is reinforced by our consumerist society, and it is deliberate. It goes back to Edward Bernays in the 1920s.

Bernays, a nephew of Sigmund Freud, has been called the "father of public relations." He was one of the key figures who worked to make people believe that if you just buy more things, you'll be happier. He was hired by presidents of the United States and major corporations to get people to think that "more is better." He brought the "sex sells" concept into advertising, creating, for example, ads that showed a man driving a convertible surrounded by beautiful women and suggesting that if people got the newest, latest, greatest thing, they'd be happier.

> **Consumer**
>
> *One who consumes more value than they produce. Because consumers focus on what they get instead of what they can give, they avoid responsibility, depend on others for their happiness, and limit the value they can create. Consumers operate in scarcity, so they view the world through a lens of poverty and limitations. They believe in luck and misfortune, not choice and accountability.*

This consumerist mindset bombards us at an unprecedented level now. With our smartphones listening to and learning about us nearly 24/7, we are constantly assailed by notifications, advertisements, and suggestions built around a corporate agenda and designed to steal our time and money. With our next purchase just one voice command or click away, consumerism has never been easier.

The corporate agenda reinforces the idea that happiness and wealth go hand in hand. And yes, it certainly makes a huge difference to have enough money to meet foundational needs and ensure basic survival, so at that level, there is a direct correlation; but survival and prosperity are two entirely different things.

Beyond basic needs, the correlation between wealth and happiness is far more variable. Expecting money to buy happiness is a very destructive drug. It's kind of like cocaine. People do cocaine, feel that peak experience for a moment, and then crash. An influx of money can be just like that: we get a hit of dopamine and feel good, but the feeling doesn't last. Neither does the money.

Being trapped in consumerism doesn't create sustainable happiness, because we always feel like we must buy the next thing. Even if we feel contented for a moment, soon enough, we meet someone who has more—a bigger business, bigger house, more money, more awards, more accolades—and the destructive cycle continues.

As a result, we get stuck in a losing game where it's always about getting, needing, or wanting more. We run as hard as we can to obtain the possessions that will lead to us being accepted and then, when we find out that someone else has more, we're right back in the same trap, no matter how much we have.

Even the definition of "having enough" has changed as we've continued to consume. Never realizing that more things don't necessarily mean a better life, we now fill sheds, storage units, and houses to overflowing with all our things. The more we have, the more we have to manage.

Money = Happiness is a sacred cow. If we believe that money is the number one reason for our happiness or unhappiness, we will never have enough; we will live a life defined by materialism and the eternal pursuit of more.

Money is a useful tool, but like many things, its virtue is ultimately determined by context. Take a hammer, for example. Is it good or bad? If it's helping me fix or build something, that's good. But if I'm using it to hurt someone, that's bad.

We have to put life and money in the proper context, which means creating a vision for our lives that's consistent with who we are at our core, rather than with what others—preachers, teachers, family, friends, corporations, governments—tell us we should do and care about.

In our gut we know what's best for us, but we're addicted to the noise of TV, podcasts, the news, and social media, all of which are telling us what will make our lives better. It's like suddenly getting emails from a source we don't remember subscribing to and automatically believing what they tell us.

Disruption is here to stay, and the consequences of unproductive and false money beliefs, systems, and practices have become even more severe.

It's time to opt out of the noise, focus on self-care, and discover and listen to your inner voice.

## KEY CONCEPTS FROM KILLING SACRED COWS

If you haven't read *Killing Sacred Cows,* or if it's been a while since you did, I'd like to give you an overview of some of the key concepts from that book. These concepts are foundational and will help you as you begin to define wealth on your own terms and let go of the beliefs, systems, and practices that don't serve you.

### The Producer Paradigm

When writing *Killing Sacred Cows,* I created an important distinction: Producer versus Consumer. In the Producer Paradigm, one creates more value than one consumes, hence the term "Producer." In the Consumer Condition, one looks to take more value than one consumes. It is born of the zero-sum game, scarcity mindset.

**Consumer Condition**

*A worldview that emphasizes scarcity, win-lose transactions, fear, selfishness, dependence, ownership, accumulation, destruction, luck, and entitlement.*

Back then, it was common to say, "just create more value." But what is the best way to create value, and how can you create it if you aren't clear about your Soul Purpose, your best skill sets, or the best platforms you can use to reach people? More effort doesn't always translate to more value. And if we become exhausted and diminished from working tirelessly to provide value, we will create less value over time. Knowing our own value, knowing the best way to create value, protecting our energy, finding time to invest in ourselves, and knowing when to say no are all critical to the equation of sustainable value. Our pursuits can be valuable in the moment but not lead to our greatest value. Our work can make us money, and even be enjoyable, but come at the cost of our health, our family, and our free time. We might be doing something that isn't really engaging the best of who we are and therefore crowding out time for discovery, skill development, and fulfillment. Know what you value and discover ways to create value consistent with the best of who you are.

Value is personal. It is a perspective. Value is different for everyone. What one person enjoys, another may feel indifferent about. What do you enjoy, what is useful and fulfilling for you? I used to say, "Just create more value," but the question becomes: how? And value for whom? And what are the obstacles preventing one from creating value?

> **Producer**
>
> *One who produces more value than he or she consumes. Producers are the responsible, innovative, and creative people who create the products and services that we buy and use. They lift, bless, serve, and contribute to the world. Producers operate in abundance, and their worldview includes limitless possibilities for value creation.*

A variety of obstacles prevent us from creating value: difficult circumstances; childhood trauma; scarcity; feelings of anger, unworthiness, frustration; or any unprocessed emotion. Jealously and envy can consume happiness and stifle creativity. This can lead to working harder to prove oneself and even adding more value, but at what cost? To what end? Someone in the Consumer Condition rarely knows that they are functioning in a way that limits their ability to create value and even pushes people away.

> **Producer Paradigm**
>
> *A worldview that emphasizes abundance, win-win interactions, faith, service, interdependence, stewardship, utilization, creation, accountability, and value creation.*

## Soul Purpose

In December, 2006, I was writing a program called Freedom FastTrack, a financial process that maps out seven stages for the creation of economic independence within ten years. While working on the second stage, I wrote "Soul Purpose Activator" and got nervous, a bit scared even. I thought, *I'm a financial guy. What am I doing writing the words "Soul Purpose"?*

But deep down, I knew that this was the missing ingredient from finance.

Soul Purpose.

Soul Purpose is who you are. It's the unique combination of your values—your script for how you operate—your abilities, and your passion. When you're living a life you love, you fully express those qualities.

More than being a Producer, life is about Soul Purpose. Your Soul Purpose informs your investments, your career, and your daily actions; if you know it, remember it and live it.

> **Soul Purpose**
>
> *Your values, passions, and abilities combined for the highest context of living; who you are when you are at your best. The highest levels of joy and fulfillment come from knowing and living your Soul Purpose.*

In my early career, being a Producer meant using any means to make more money than was spent. But what if you aren't doing something that sings to your soul, challenges you, or brings you satisfaction and fulfillment? Not all work will pay huge financial dividends, and not all actions have to lead to a monetary payoff, but in the big picture of quality of life, Soul Purpose counts.

Who are you?

What do you really what?

In the absence of fear and scarcity, what would you choose to do? How would you live?

These can be difficult questions when someone is hungry and behind on bills. But they can also be difficult when someone is making money doing something that brings them no joy. Soul Purpose is more than what you do; it is who you are when you are at your best, fully self-expressed. With all the fears and worry, doubt and the quest for social acceptance, finding Soul Purpose has become more complicated.

With so many options, which do you choose?

With so many voices, whose should you listen to?

What path will lead you to societal success?

Societal success (money, awards, accolades) and Soul Purpose are not mutually exclusive, but the pursuit of societal success can be a detour or damaging to one's life journey when outcome takes priority over experience, making money crowds out enjoyment, or comparison takes priority over compassion and contentment. You may have heard the famous quotation "Comparison is the thief of joy." (The origin of this quotation is unknown, though it is most often attributed to Theodore Roosevelt.) If money is the only scorecard, there is always someone with more.

Being a Producer is a natural by-product of knowing and living your Soul Purpose. In the absence of Soul Purpose, distractions look like opportunities and there is never time to be present, celebrate, or pause. When you're in the grind—chasing money, paying off debt, trying to find significance in net worth—you experience minimal enjoyment. Being a Producer is about producing the most value for others consistent with who you are, but if you aren't clear about who you are, busyness ensues as you jump from project to project and opportunity to opportunity. Before you work to create more value, discover your value.

Bring an abundance of compassion and forgiveness to the process of healing the wounds inflicted by those who doubted, rejected, or harmed you. If you were taught to ignore your feelings or simply don't have the ability to deal with difficult situations because of wounds you sustained— especially at a young age—this will inevitably impact how you deal with money, how you view money.

A healthy relationship with money requires work that most people have never considered: healing unprocessed pain and trauma, specifically from childhood. Doing this work will not only transform your relationship to money, it will also transform your life.

> **Before you work to create more value, discover your value.**

We all have pain. We all have trauma to heal. But if our pain remains hidden or ignored, it leads to escapism or even addiction. Unresolved childhood issues undermine the potential for prosperity. Without facing these issues, our perspective and the way we operate in the world are, at a minimum, limited—or worse, destructive.

The way you treat money can be directly related to the stories you told yourself in the most difficult moments of growing up. Yes, the amount money you earn, keep, and have the ability to invest can be massively influenced by your relationship to moments, people, and tough situations from childhood. This can cause some people to chase money. Others spend it recklessly. Some may obsess about saving it. Our financial maturity can be stunted by moments when our brain was still developing and we created artificial stories, myths that remain buried in our unconscious minds and manifest in how we relate to money.

You can never earn, spend, or save enough to outrun the scarcity mindset created when you felt unsafe as a child. Net worth isn't powerful enough to heal those wounds. Owning more elaborate and elegant things can't fill the void. Healing begins with removing the myths, lies, and limitations from the past so you can start with a blank slate.

Produce in a way that is consistent with what brings you fulfillment and joy.

Rather than trying to please everyone else, or getting caught in a trap of consumerism, ask:

Who am I?

What do I really want?

What is worthy of my time?

What would it take for me to build the life I love?

What is it that matters most to me?

What makes me feel fulfilled?

What is *my* purpose?

## REAL RETIREMENT

When we focus on being Producers and living our Soul Purpose, we can start to redefine retirement. Rather than retire from work—which sometimes includes retiring from life—build the life you don't want to retire from. This is a new way to view retirement.

You may think, *I'm going to live in scarcity my whole life so I can have abundance when I retire.* No. You have established the habit of scarcity thinking, which numbs you to life.

Don't retire from life. Retire from sacrifice. Retire from people-pleasing at your own expense. Retire from the zero-sum, competition-driven scarcity game. Find meaningful work and continue on the path of value creation.

As of this writing, the pandemic continues to leave its mark on our lives and our emotions. It has created some sacred cows of its own. It has become a great excuse—an excuse to be disconnected, an excuse for why things didn't happen that we wanted to happen, an excuse for lack of customer service or for not keeping our word.

Let's go through those feelings and ask, are they serving us? The future of the economy is hard to predict, but it's easy to predict the outcomes of our current beliefs and behavior. What will the results of living in scarcity be? Discontentment, frustration, broken relationships, negative internal dialogue, and blaming external factors, like artificial intelligence, pandemics, governments, and corporations. Those complaints might be valid, but do they serve us and allow us to get where we want to go?

In order to plant new seeds that sprout in the garden of humanity, remove the weeds—the news, negative people (whom we can love from a distance), self-hatred, self-doubt, and unprocessed emotions.

It is time to allow a little light in. So, what brings you light? What relationships and people inspire you? What do you do that makes you feel inspired? Is it handwriting notes that you send to express gratitude? Is it hugging someone or telling them that you love them? Where can you forgive yourself or others? Take this moment for a little win-accounting and acknowledge what you have already accomplished.

What if part of our purpose is just to take care of ourselves for a bit? And what if part of that is just finding something that we enjoy doing?

Your Soul Purpose can sprout and the sun can break through, but you have to add water; you have to do certain things on a regular basis to find your flow.

I have a cabin near a river. There is so much life that comes from that river, so many things that happen because of that flow.

We've got to find our flow. Unlock all of who you are by removing censorship, negative self-talk, and fear to find your own flow.

Fear is a weed that diminishes who we are. When we choose love over fear, when we choose progress over perfection, we can rise above fear.

## Chapter Two

# The Missing Ingredient

PURPOSE CAN FEEL ELUSIVE OR HARD TO DEFINE AT THE BEST of times. And in times of disruption, chaos, or a global pandemic, purpose can get crowded out, pushed to the side, or overlooked entirely. In today's world, it is easy to become dissociated and fall into meaningless escapism. Changes in the economy, our health, or quarantines that separate us—throwing off daily routines, rhythms and interactions—can create feelings of isolation and hopelessness.

**Escapism**

*Distractions or detours designed to delay meaningful moments. Escapism prevents us from being present and advocates for numbing out when we're uncomfortable, overwhelmed, or in a scarcity mindset.*

In these times, it is imperative that we become more intentional, even diligent, to avoid becoming victims of circumstance and losing our time, or even the very essence of our being, to escapism.

What if you opted out of complaining about politics and opted in to daily meditation and contemplation of your life's purpose?

What if you turned off the news and tuned into your intuition instead?

What if, rather than getting caught up in the hustle and bustle of the world, you took time for a hobby or to pause and think?

What if you used the time you spent in escapism to heal instead—to face your fears, process your pain, and let go of limiting beliefs that cloud the future—*your* future? This can happen in a conversation you have been putting off or in addressing an issue you have yet to face. It can even happen in a letter you write taking responsibility, asking for forgiveness, and choosing to express love.

In this new world and its ever-changing economy, what if you focused on the things you can control, the things that lead to a better life for you and those you love? In a time when most are fighting and complaining, can you focus instead on changing your habits, defining your win, and creating your vision? You can if you address escapism.

Escapism is one of the most common sacred cows. It robs us of our time, destroys prosperity and prevents us from living our Soul Purpose.

Escapism comes from a sense of hopelessness, which steals momentum and progress. When the world feels heavy, escapism leads to thoughts like, *I just can't deal with life, work, friends, family, finances, projects, goals,* etc. So instead of dealing with things or facing our obstacles, we look for outlets that will let us escape them. It's easier to get caught up in the problems and drama of a TV series, for example, than it is to examine ourselves, our lives, and our relationships.

Feeling overwhelmed can lead to hiding from our problems through overuse of social media, playing video games, gambling, drinking, overeating, even sleeping too much. Again, it's about context. These things can be fun or useful on occasion, but when they become an excuse, a place to hide, or a way to numb ourselves, we delay the inevitable, making matters worse. These outlets, these distractions, are promoted and in our faces more now than ever before, perpetuating fear, reinforcing damaging beliefs, and creating an addiction to what is wrong with the world, to the nonstop negativity that keeps us all scared, angry, and divided.

The news isn't something people tune into at five or nine p.m. anymore. It's there 24/7, constantly whispering in our ears about the worst of what is happening in every corner of the earth. In this cycle of noise and negativity, emotion is no longer our own. Instead of taking the time to process our feelings, we get instantly angry about narratives created by correspondents posing as journalists, or are lured away by clickbait headlines that steal our focus and keep us from reaching our full potential. Our Soul Purpose.

Escapism has no time for our emotions. When we indulge in escapism, we hold our emotions in, push them down, and just get sadder and lonelier, more confused, frustrated, and isolated. We do everything we can to avoid pain, which often leads to us doing or feeling nothing at all. This is how escapism holds us captive.

The missing ingredient to financial independence is healing the trauma and wounds from our childhoods. You may be thinking that trauma and financial stress are unrelated. You may want to skip this chapter and get to "the good stuff." Please stay with me. *Killing Sacred Cows* changed the game for so many people, including me. And yet it wasn't until I started healing childhood pain that I truly gained financial freedom.

Trauma we experience in childhood creates habits that prevent us from detecting sacred cows and living our Soul Purpose. When we try to avoid experiencing that pain, we live unexamined lives where sacred cows continue to rule. When we hide pain from ourselves—*I never want to feel that again* or *I never want to experience that again*—we numb out, disconnect, and find ways to escape reality, all in the name of "protection." Unfortunately, that protection keeps us from being present, diminishes our expression and ability to connect, and even keeps us from experiencing joy.

If we do the work to recognize these subconscious beliefs and patterns that originated in childhood (when we didn't have the know-how or brain capacity to properly deal with traumatic incidents), we can use compassion to begin to heal.

## YOUR PAIN DOESN'T HAVE TO BE "EXTREME"

Some people grow up in difficult environments and circumstances, but if the pain from those formative years goes unprocessed, or we learn the wrong lessons and become skeptical, it can impact our future behavior and, as I mentioned in the previous chapter, show up in our relationship with money. Some people are dealing with extreme examples from child-hood, like homelessness or abuse. But even seemingly insignificant situations can have a lasting negative impact.

Here's an example. One time, my mom said, "I want you to take a nap."

Now, I was a little kid, and I didn't want to take a nap, so she said, "Okay, I'll come lie down by you." It was great. I felt safe and slept like a baby.

But when I woke up, she was gone. She had left to go to work, but I didn't realize that. I felt completely abandoned. I was just a little kid; being so young, I didn't understand the difference between my mom leaving forever and just going to work to provide for our family. Because this incident is so insignificant in the eyes of the world, I didn't share it for a long time. Yet because I did not address it and discounted it as insignificant, I continued to feel its impact and had an irrational fear of being abandoned.

At other times in my childhood, I experienced more extreme situations.

One occurred when I was three years old. My mom went for a walk, and I followed her on my Big Wheel tricycle. As she stopped to speak to a friend, I tried to cross the street by myself—just in time to get hit by a car going at full speed.

I remember that when I got up, I was crying so hard I couldn't see and ended up accidentally running to the woman who hit me, thinking it was my mom. Luckily, a police meeting was taking place a block away and an officer quickly arrived on the scene and rushed us, sirens blazing, to the hospital (which was more than thirty miles away).

As the cop raced toward the hospital, I bled and hyperventilated in my mom's arms. To make matters worse, she was pregnant with my little sister. It was the first time I remember seeing my mom in fear.

After getting my stitches, I was wheeled into a hospital room filled with my family members. My dad had shown up in full coal-mining gear, with black coal dust on his face, and my grandparents came rushing in as well. In those moments, I really saw firsthand how fragile life could be—but despite everyone being there for me and loving me unconditionally, I still had the thought: *If I am not perfect, I hurt the ones I love.*

Another incident took place when I was five years old. Whenever I spent time with my grandparents, I always headed to the creek behind their house. It was one of my favorite places in the world. There, in my happy place, I created bike jumps, built racetracks, collected salamanders, skipped rocks, and just lost track of time.

Then, one day, two older boys showed up. They approached me and asked if I wanted to be initiated into their club. I was excited and flattered by the older boys' attention at first, but then they asked me to pull down my pants.

I don't remember much about what happened next, but I do recall trying to race away on my bike, hitting a bump, and crushing my ribs into the handlebars before finally toppling over the bike. I was left with a bloody nose, a scraped-up elbow, and some mean bruises.

When my parents finally came to pick me up and asked what happened, my only reply was, "Oh, nothing really, just wrecked my bike." It was the first time I remember lying to them, hiding something from them.

The second two stories are obviously extreme examples, and it wasn't until I acknowledged, worked through, and processed these incidents that I was able to transform my relationship with money and improve my overall well-being. For me as a kid, waking up from a nap to find my mom gone was not much different, emotionally, from the much more difficult and complex traumas.

Since we don't always remember what happens to us in childhood—forgetting is often a protection mechanism—we may be held captive by limiting beliefs.

When we are children, our brains have yet to fully develop, and it may be hard to make sense of difficulties and trauma. If we don't take the time to look back and examine our childhoods as adults, we learn the wrong lessons and undermine our ability to love, accept support, or process our pain. All of this leads to scarcity.

Some people don't remember anything from childhood because it was so damaging to their psyche. Many are now living lives in which they don't feel fulfillment or joy and are either trying to hold on to what they've got or chasing unachievable futures at the expense of today—hence our unfulfilled, consumerist world that lacks happiness and peace of mind. When we learn the wrong lessons, we form limited beliefs.

It is time to heal, time to disrupt that system and recognize that, first of all, we're all lovable *as we are.*

Yes, you are lovable. All of who you are.

The good and the bad. The glory and the imperfections.

Yes, even the mistakes. We all make mistakes, but your mistakes don't make you. They make you more human. And they certainly don't make you less lovable, because love has no prerequisite and requires no accomplishment. We can all just choose it, and it's the most abundant resource available.

You may be thinking, *Why are we talking so much about love in a money book?* It's because, with love, we can start to heal. You see, many people confuse love and money. They believe that when there is enough money, then they'll be happy. Then they'll be okay. Then they'll be lovable.

Rather than chasing money, numbing out, or escaping when difficult circumstances and stories are happening, try taking time for some personal reflection, forgiveness, and doing the simple things that can lead to extraordinary results. This will not only impact your happiness; it will also impact your relationship with money, because money cannot make up for the pain experienced in childhood or misguided beliefs about our own value.

We expect money to do what it was never designed or intended to do: make us feel happy, validated, and like we're enough. We want money in order to feel worthy, to feel valued—but in the absence of love and the presence of scarcity, there is no win.

It is when we haven't accepted ourselves, when we lack gratitude or understanding, that we turn to money to save us, to be the story of who we are or are not. But no rate of return, no amount of savings, luck, discipline, or net worth, will ever bring us lasting happiness.

## HEALING THE CHILD

To start the process of healing, look at the times when you were young that you've tucked away due to the pain and secretly promised you'd never bring up again. These moments become powerful myths. They create false beliefs that govern your future actions and disrupt your current ability to be present and experience peace of mind.

As children, we do not have the brain development or proper tools to handle these scary or difficult scenarios, but if left unprocessed or hidden in our psyches, they manifest as limitations, doubt, or chaos throughout adulthood. Unchecked myths from childhood can create a lingering sense of victimhood and cause the patterns and stories of our current frustrations and setbacks.

Our brains recognize—and even predict—similar outcomes decades later. Even though we may be equipped to handle situations in an entirely different way as adults, our ability to cope is stunted by early traumas and childhood programming. These moments fuel scarcity in the present as remnants and reminders highlighting potential failure. Ultimately, they hold us back.

You see, when we identify or define ourselves by our past mistakes or view the world as a dangerous and terrifying place, we limit our capacity to love and enjoy life. We hold ourselves back from growth and stay trapped in the patterns that prevent our fulfillment and cloud our ability to see our own value.

It is in these times of worry and stress that our childhood issues can come back to haunt us. We may have the bodies of adults, but without healing those critical, developmental moments, early programming takes over and we resort to coping with our issues like children.

## TIME FOR A HEALING CONVERSATION

When most people cry, their immediate reaction is to apologize for it. However they frame the apology, what they're really saying is:

"I'm sorry for letting you see how I really feel."

"I'm sorry for being vulnerable right now."

"I'm sorry that this might be uncomfortable."

Healing may include tears, so there's no need to apologize for them. The only thing to forgive in that moment is the unfair judgment you place on yourself.

When you feel sadness, depression, anger, or frustration, ask yourself, *When did I first feel this way? What is my earliest memory of this happening? What was going on? What triggered it?* Maybe, at that time, you felt that something wasn't right, or that you were alone or had no voice. When we go back and really examine our childhoods, we realize that all the adult effort and money in the world will not bring us prosperity and sustained happiness until healing takes place.

I began to transform my own childhood trauma by first having a conversation with my five-year-old self. I held a picture of myself at that age in my hand, and with all the gratitude and love of the adult I had become, I let that kid know that everything was going to be okay, that I am okay. This helped me to address the childhood wounds that had held power over me and my choices and begin to heal.

So, what would you say? How would you talk to your five-year-old self to let that child know who you truly are today, that what happened in your youth was not your fault, and that you can replace your judgment, fear, and worry with love and forgiveness?

Go get a picture of yourself, from your own childhood.

Look at it. How cute were you?

Probably adorable.

Now ask yourself, *Would I ever hit this kid?*

Would you blame this sweet face for all your current failures?

Would you ever say the mean things that you're saying about yourself today (in your head) to this five-year-old?

No, of course not.

My awkward yet impactful conversation took time. I kept using the language of an adult and it was uncomfortable, but after a few attempts, I was able to really communicate like I would to an actual five-year-old. It went something like this:

"Hey, bud, we got this. It's okay. We made it. You did the best you knew how. You didn't know that was going to happen; it wasn't your fault. It's okay. You are loved. You are safe!"

As I was going through all of this, I had the biggest breakthrough and started bawling. It was early in the morning and the sound of my sobs woke up my wife, who saw tears rolling down my cheeks and asked if everything was okay.

It was beyond okay. It was my first step on the path of healing.

## HEALING WILL HELP YOU WEATHER FINANCIAL STORMS

I didn't know about the disruptive impact of these childhood issues when I wrote *Killing Sacred Cows*. Before I worked on my childhood, I tried to use income to heal my wounds and prove that I was worthy. I thought that if I made enough, I was something, I could be loved. But this was a black hole. There was never enough money because money couldn't fix the issue.

> **Net Worth**
>
> A person's financial assets minus his or her liabilities. Net worth is removed from income in that a person could theoretically have a net worth of $1 million and have no income. Net worth is a function of a person's balance sheet.

When my self-worth was no longer tied to my net worth, I discovered space for joy and fun. I spent more time with my family and friends, established and renewed traditions, explored hobbies, and learned new skills. And I was rewarded with a broader vision, a renewed sense of purpose, and more confidence. I realized that I had been letting my five-year-old mentality run my adult life. When I removed my obsession with seeking value through more money, I learned to feel abundant enough to say no to work and investments that did not serve me. Money became *a* consideration, not *the* consideration.

My life changed.

Having a new vision gave me purpose and drive during a time when complaining and fear was the norm—in 2020, for example. It allowed me to ask for support and invest in relationships at a different level. I stopped investing in anything outside of my business or skill sets. This allowed me to double down on my business and have more time for my family and more control over my schedule. Instead of reading spreadsheets, responding to managers of my properties, and talking to attorneys about legal entities for my partnerships, I spend time in co-creation and collaboration.

I see money as a by-product of service, and service as a by-product of Soul Purpose. Now, my Soul Purpose is sacred. I stick to what I know, to what is most fulfilling. I consistently ask myself if my calendar represents who I want to be. Rather than question if I have enough money to feel worthy, I ask myself, *Am I living a life of love?*

With this profound change, I am free from the impact of the newest trends, disruptions, and downturns. I have stability. I don't get dragged into the scarcity thinking that is perpetuated and exaggerated by the media. I have more liquidity, which means I can act quickly; my money is not tied up in retirement plans. Rather than hope for the best, I am economically independent. I can say yes to things that develop me as a person without worrying if I can pay the bills. In times of disruption, I can be of service when other people are stuck.

> **Rather than question if I have enough money to feel worthy, I ask myself, Am I living a life of love?**

The government and corporations cannot save us. Your happiness begins with you, your perspective, and learning from your past rather than being held captive by it. Again, it begins with responsibility. Have compassion. Choose love.

## THE POWER OF THE PAUSE

The world is filled with distractions. This busyness limits our ability to listen to our own intuition. While we listen to so many others, we rarely listen to ourselves.

Intuition is subtle but powerful. It comes in the quiet moments, not in when your world is noisy. How much of your day do you spend in silence? Do you take time to think, or to listen to yourself?

Consider starting your day with a little morning tuning. For some, this is meditation, time for gratitude, or quiet time. You may want to write down a modest intention for the day or reinforce, in writing, what you are capable of. Take time to reflect on the previous day: what went well with it, and what might you choose to improve upon moving forward? The game changer is carving out time for your hobby or creative practice. What allows you to lose track of time or reduce stress that may have nothing to do with money, just enjoyment?

As for exercise, consider starting with something like walking or stretching if you aren't currently working out. Progress over perfection—just start somewhere. If you want more motivation, you can always sign up for a race or competition, but only if that really calls to you. The key is to do something consistently, on a daily basis, to invite better health into your life. Start your day by investing in yourself. Create space to design your life. Find time for yourself. Take this time to connect with *you*. Hit pause. Reevaluate, reexamine, and reclaim the best of who you are.

Escapism and sacrifice obscure the saboteur of prosperity, our unprocessed pain. Pain can be like a puppet master, pulling at the strings of escapism. It leads to predictable, limited results. I can predict most of someone's future results or limitations depending on whether or not they have unprocessed pain. This pain prevents prosperity and replaces it with addiction, disconnection, and sometimes even disease. Pain becomes like a pressure cooker of sadness and sorrow, anger and angst, frustration and depression. If we don't deal with our pain, that outcome is inevitable. But if we face our pain and feel our emotions, connection is on the other side.

Pain comes from many sources—our experiences, our environment, and those we love.

Requiring external factors to determine our happiness is narcissistic. This kind of narcissism may seem noble. I've thought, *If my wife isn't happy, that's my fault, and I've got to do everything I can to make my kids happy.* But in trying to save them from pain, I was diminishing and censoring them; they didn't want to tell me if they felt pain, because they didn't want to worry me.

As my acting coach Larry Moss likes to remind me, worry is a terrible use of the imagination. It isolates us and prevents us from processing our emotions because it doesn't lead to connection—it leads to imagining all the worst-case scenarios, all the reasons why something seems impossible.

When we have any emotion, it's great to feel it, experience it. There can be power in expressing it by venting, but it has to be the kind of venting that leads to something positive. Use a "safe container," or what I call "The Trust Tree." Find someone you trust and ask for a space, a safe container in which to process your emotions. Rather than suppressing the emotions and pretending they don't exist, feel them, express them, and let them through. Then, at the end of this time, make a commitment to do something about what is causing them. There is real freedom in expressing your emotions versus hiding from them.

Facing your pain, being present, and loving yourself begins with knowing you're not broken; you just haven't processed your pain. Pain is part of life, part of the human experience. There is much in our lives that is beyond our control. But if we can process our experiences with love and compassion, especially for ourselves, we can get to the other side and find what we've always been looking for: knowledge of who we are and why we're here.

# Chapter Three

# What Game Are You Playing?

S CARCITY COMES FROM OUR PAIN OR IS HANDED DOWN TO US by the people we know and love. That pain comes from past experience and is reinforced by the *I'm not enough, I'm not lovable, I can't do this* feeling.

Scarcity is why people turn to the world and say, "Will you take care of me? Will the government step in? Will someone else do it for me?"

If we're looking for happiness in a spouse, child, company, or community, we've already lost the game.

People get trapped in scarcity in different ways. The good news is, there is a better way to play—one where you win before you begin.

## PLAYING NOT TO LOSE

The first side of the scarcity coin is a trap I call "playing not to lose." I inherited this idea from my great-grandfather, who came from San Giovanni in Fiore, a small, desolate town in southern Italy. When I visited this town a few years ago, I understood why he left in the early 1900s. He had to find a better way to provide for his family. His wife was pregnant with their first child, but he couldn't make ends meet. He, his dad, and his half-brother hiked through the mountains to a port and came to America. They heard that in central Utah, some Greeks and Italians were making good money working in coal mines. They got there just in time for a mining disaster that killed over a hundred people.

My great-grandfather became a goatherd and shepherd until the mines reopened. He lived in a tent while he worked to save up enough money to buy a house and move his wife and daughter from Italy to Sunnyside, Utah. It took him years to finally see his wife again and meet his seven-year-old daughter for the first time. This extreme circumstance shaped his view of the world, one of sacrifice and playing not to lose.

What we believe today can determine how our families operate for generations to come. When we come from place of scarcity, it limits results, creates stress, and prevents us from reaching our fullest potential.

My family is very fiscally conservative. They grew up setting aside as much money as possible and were always concerned about the prices of things. They just wanted to do what was best; it was all they knew. But they were trapped in a losing game.

I inherited that attitude. I started my first business when I was fifteen and saved every dollar I made. I was such a cheapskate that once, when I was driving and hungry, I bought a seven-dollar bag of jerky on the side of the road and regretted the purchase for months. This is how I had been trained to think, and what I thought would create safety and stability.

That's "play not to lose": hold it because someone else might want to take it. Take it before someone else does. Always budget and look for ways to eliminate costs.

## PLAYING TO WIN

The other side of the scarcity coin is playing to win. You may remember the board game called *Life*. Do you remember the number one move that you had to make to win? If you made this one move right in the beginning, you were likely to win. If you didn't, you never won. It was going to college: you've got to get a college degree. That's planted in people's minds right now. You'll get a $250,000 student loan because *Life* taught that you had to get a college degree to win. *Monopoly* is similar. We get our notion of capitalism from *Monopoly:* take, take, take. Get Park Place and Broadway. Play to win.

The play-to-win side of the scarcity coin comes, in part, from these types of games. The mantra: hustle, grind, and work. Playing to win is only about the future, never enjoying the present—more, bigger, better, faster. It leads to discontent. Yes, you might have something resembling wealth, but, like playing not to lose, playing to win leads to the disastrous results of not being present, sacrificing, and delaying.

Playing to win may create more material progress than playing not to lose, but neither approach creates the space for enjoying the process along the way. For years, my excuse was that I was working so hard for my family, that my traveling and working constantly was to provide for them. But that was a sacred cow, a lie. I was doing it because I was trying to prove my worth. I was caught in the trappings of success at the expense of my life, my family.

No matter how much you have, there is always more to get when you play to win. There is always someone who is doing better or has more; there is always more to be done. There is no room for pause, celebration, or living a life you love.

There's an Adam Sandler movie called *Click*. In it, Sandler's character has a remote control that allows him to fast-forward through life events. He tries to fast-forward through his pain; then he realizes he's an old man and has missed out on all of his experiences.[1] If we continue to believe that if we sacrifice now, then one day, someday, it will all pay off, or that the ends justify the means, we lose in the same way: fast-forwarding to the next goal, the next project or dollar.

This isn't so different from the concept of retirement: work hard and save money so you can finally afford to do the things you love when you might be too old to do them, and miss out on memories along the way. You put money away in a retirement account, and finally, when you're sixty-five, you can enjoy it—if the market cooperates. But where did this notion of retirement come from? From the last century, when people worked until they died—seven days a week, in dangerous environments.

Hustling so you can eventually afford an amazing life is playing to win. What about your health, your hobbies, and the memories you rob yourself of along the way?

## THE BETTER WAY TO PLAY

There is a different approach, which I call "Win Then Play." You win before you begin. If you establish your vision and the rules for how you'll execute it on your terms, you win. The win is in the work. The win is in creating a life you don't want to fast-forward through or retire from.

What matters to you? What do you want each day to look like? Vision is not something to be copied, but something to be created—consistent with your Soul Purpose.

When the end justifies the means, we lose joy in the journey; if it is only about the outcome, and we begrudgingly trade away our lives to achieve the promise of a destination, we lose. When our happiness depends on variables we don't control, we lose.

So, know your win before you begin. What do you control? How can you enjoy the process along the way? What game do you want to play, and how do you want to play it? What is on your list of dos and don'ts? What do you enjoy, and what would you rather not do? Where can you delegate? Which opportunities aren't worth the cost?

Again, what's your win? If you didn't have the stress of obligations like debt or the pressure of external values and expectations, what would you want simply because it makes you feel fulfilled? This is how we get beyond sacred cows: we create the game for ourselves.

Some people don't allow for this type of thinking because they believe (erroneously) that it is selfish. But we're the best we can be when we're personally fulfilled because we no longer feel lack. We fuel our energy when we take care of ourselves, and part of that is finding the artist inside, the art of creating our lives. We don't have to do what the world deems valuable. It's what *we* find valuable, expressive, and energy-giving that matters. Expression over perfection—this will help us get past the sacred cows. This will help us heal. This will help us to process the pain.

Be the artist of your life. What do you want to paint into existence on your blank canvas? What hobbies do you enjoy? When do you feel most creative and joyful? When you discover your flow, you will find that the more you give, the more you *can* give. Your capacity for creation expands. It begins with you, establishing a game that's worth playing and winning, building a game and a life that you love.

## WHAT GAME ARE YOU PLAYING?

When I talk about games, it might seem like I'm discounting the value of life. But we learn through games. When we think of something as a game, it seems more fun and not as stressful. When we think of business, or work, we often slide down the slope of sacrifice. Why not create in a spirit of fun? How would you create your game if you could do it any way you wanted?

We do get to invent our games; in fact, we're all inventors in how we live life—our actions and reactions, what we choose to do or not do, what we stand for or stand against.

Change the game, raise the stakes, and choose to go all in. What is your game?

For example, my little sister is a teacher. Teachers are not known to make a lot of money, but she created a game: her blog. The blog is about how to engage students in a fun way, like having them wear costumes when they're learning about a particular subject. She found a way to win at teaching that fills her with purpose and joy. Her blog became the second most visited blog in teaching. She's making more money from it than from her salary. My sister won a Teacher of the Year award in her school district when she was in her early thirties because she brought her game to life.

You write the game of your life. In fact, your life depends on your writing it, but most people succumb to the "If you want this, you've got to sacrifice that" mentality. My game begins with the blank slate, with no sacrifice.

What do you enjoy? What feels playful to you? That will be work that's worth doing (even if it doesn't feel like play in every moment). When you pursue your vision, you win every moment you work on it. If you happen to receive awards or accolades, they are simply gravy. The game is the win.

## CREATE MORE RELATIONSHIP CAPITAL

We've been taught that in games, especially sports, there's a winner and a loser. But I prefer to think in terms of what I call "the divinity of diversity." We all have different perspectives and preferences. What we enjoy, others do not. We're effective in areas where others are not. This gives us a reason to exchange with one another, to collaborate rather than isolate. As we unfold that possibility, we can experience wins all over the finding-our-purpose game board. Others' purposes differ from ours, which gives us a chance to be wealthier together.

Thinking that if you want something done right, you've got to do it yourself comes from a scarcity mentality. If you want something done right, you'd better collaborate. Collaboration builds Relationship Capital—the mentors, family, friends, networks, and organizations that highlight and amplify the best of who you are and help you realize your vision. These people are your hidden assets. When you're around them, you co-create on a different level. You see this sometimes in sports when a team leader unlocks the potential of the players.

How many people have you known who felt they were invisible, who wanted to be seen and heard? You have the power to help people by listening to them, acknowledging them, and encouraging them. These are the keys to unlocking potential in humanity, potential the people you interact with might not even have known was there.

We want our assets to appreciate; that is, we want them to increase in value. We increase the value of our relationships by appreciating them. Try sending a handwritten note. Sending someone a note to acknowledge who they are in your life can build Relationship Capital.

You can support people in conversation by asking them good questions. I used to ask people how I could create the most value, but then I realized that this was a limiting question. Instead, I cultivated clarity by asking them questions like, "What's your biggest challenge?" "What's your biggest opportunity?" "What projects are you doing?" "What are you most excited about?"

Take the time to have quality conversations and find out what is happening in people's lives. Listen attentively: you might be able to connect them with relationships that could take their lives to a new level. Or you might be able to offer solutions to problems they're struggling with.

The three things that rob people of vision are the feeling that there isn't enough money, the feeling that there isn't enough time, and the feeling that there isn't enough ability. But these things are only true in isolation, when you're trying to do too much alone. They are almost never true in collaboration. You can collaborate with others to create more value and build Relationship Capital.

Recently, I made two connections over the phone. I referred a good friend to my cryptocurrency consultant and to someone who is great at investing. It took no time. I'm not looking for compensation; I simply help people make connections because I enjoy doing it. I also enjoy buying books for people and sending them along with handwritten notes. Building Relationship Capital can also involve giving someone a hug, making them a latte, or inviting them for a meal.

Author Stephen R. Covey talks about making deposits into an emotional bank account before you make withdrawals.[2] There is joy to be found in supporting someone else. Don't discount any act, no matter how tiny; it might have a ripple effect on someone's heart that you could never imagine.

But here's the secret: when you allow other people to serve you, you're not making withdrawals, you're building relationships. Part of the winning game is knowing how to help people help you. You can overcome the constraints of time and money if you allow for support. Make deposits into Relationship Capital before you make withdrawals, but allow for others to add value, solve problems, and serve you as well.

## BUILD MENTAL CAPITAL

Another hidden asset is Mental Capital—knowledge, wisdom, insights, and strategies. Building Mental Capital can happen in conversation and through reading, listening, and doing. Create conditions that support the development of your Mental Capital by doing some basic things, like getting enough water and sleep.

To develop Mental Capital, remove clutter, commit to fewer things, and spend time with people you know will help you think at the highest levels. Be intentional about spending more time with people who bring out the very best in you. Look for the ways you learn best and create the space to invest in yourself regularly.

## CREATE YOUR WINNING GAME

Your winning game is within reach, but win first: know your win. Create a life you don't want to retire from. Regardless of your resources or your financial situation, you can win by following this formula.

Begin with *co-creation:* find one other person who can support and inspire you—someone who can help you move beyond the scarcity mindset and into value creation by bringing accountability.

> **Value Creation**
>
> *Identifying what others value and providing it to them.*

The next step is the *elimination* of escapism—the ways you detach or dissociate from what you want most. When you address escapism by processing your pain with love and compassion, you'll find connection and experience expanded consciousness. Having one-on-one support from a mentor or a respected peer will help you to identify and move beyond escapism.

Next, it's about *delegation*. As you build personal or professional momentum, you can start to offload tasks to people who want to do them. You can compensate them by any number of means, including gratitude, acknowledgment, and, of course, money.

Then there's *collaboration*. As you find people with competencies different from your own and involve them in your game, you'll be able to focus on what you do best, have more impact, and accomplish more.

Vision is the winning game. Without it, we engage in activity, not productivity; we become busy, but ineffective. Ultimately, vision informs our philosophy and our philosophy informs our actions.

Vision is the win. Value is the road by which that vision reaches people. Dollars are the by-product of that value, and prosperity becomes our way of being. Vision always involves co-creation, elimination, delegation, and collaboration.

## YOU ARE ALREADY WORTHY

People have a hard time understanding that they have certain gifts because they tend to focus on what is lacking. Society convinces us that we've got to sacrifice, work for years, and put in our 10,000 hours so that, one day, we'll be worthy of success. But we're already worthy. When we remove such obstacles and find our Soul Purpose, we start to see accelerated results.

The seed of prosperity can break through the soil, but most people give up before it sprouts because they get distracted. They hear about someone who made money and try to mimic patterns that may have nothing to do with their own Soul Purpose. Rather than taking time to create a vision and engage their best abilities, they are tempted by immediate gratification. *This person went from zero to a million in a day. When is that going to happen for me?*

This faulty thinking says, "Give me fame for nothing!" No, that's not the process, because you've skipped the win. The win is in the work. The win is in the process. The win is in the game, not at the end of the game.

Making money at the expense of Soul Purpose does not lead to fulfillment but is a destructive distraction that takes us off course to pursue profits without purpose. The habits of trading time for money and doing things we hate for a false promise of a better future become a philosophy of sacrifice. We chase a dollar in a direction that moves us away from fulfillment, believing the lie that more is better, all while robbing ourselves of time spent with those we love, doing what we love.

## DISTRACTION OR OPPORTUNITY?

In Chapter Six, I explain Investor DNA. Before I understood this concept, I went through a real estate crisis. I spent more than half of my time doing things I didn't enjoy. I dreaded dealing with property managers, tenants, banks, attorneys, and spreadsheets. Many of the books I read and "gurus" I studied taught real estate as the best path to wealth. For me, it was the best path to being overleveraged and overextended, with over a hundred properties. Originally, I had partners handling the aspects I didn't enjoy, but due to a downturn in the real estate market, most of them went bankrupt.

It was through this disruption that I solidified some of the most important and impactful philosophies in this book, and it was the ultimate test of the concepts shared in *Killing Sacred Cows*. It led me to ask new questions about leverage, risk management, and what it meant to be a good investor.

**Investor**

> One who possesses the ability to contribute to investments and create favorable conditions for returns on those investments; mitigate their risk; build an exit strategy that allows them to profit under different circumstances; and practice the theories of utilization, acceleration, and velocity as opposed to accumulation. True investors don't invest in anything if they don't know how to make it productive.

My real estate crisis was a difficult time in my life. I asked myself, *Am I a failure? Are my wife and kids better off without me?*

I had terrible thoughts about myself. Although I never got to the point of attempting suicide, I had suicidal thoughts. My hair turned gray and I gained weight. I wasn't loving toward people, and I was irritable with those who mattered most to me. Now I can look back at this period and say, "I learned a lot." I thought my real estate investments were opportunities, but they were distractions, detours from my purpose. The only benefit was making money. I was wrapped up in a losing game until I opted out and asked myself, *What is my winning game?*

> **Cash Flow**
>
> *The combination of the amount of net income a person receives, how that income is produced, and its level of sustainability. Healthy cash flows are created by investing in tangible assets such as real estate, or more abstract assets such as intellectual property. Cash flow can be measured on an income statement.*

I love to learn, create content, and challenge myself by delivering keynotes, doing comedy, and performing one-man-shows. Investing doesn't have to mean dealing with stock, bonds, or real estate. My investments became a different type of property: intellectual property.

I do some real estate, but only when it is aligned with my win. I win when I play. This realization led to my purchase of a cabin, a music studio, and land with a river and a pond. It was time to retire from being a landlord and live in or use the property I had purchased. Even if the real estate had continued to appreciate and create cash flow, I didn't enjoy it. It might be a good investment for some, but it is not the path for me. What is your path? What is fulfilling to you?

## INVEST IN YOURSELF

Having been in finance for a few decades, people ask me about where they should invest. Which stock should they pick? The answer is simple. You should pick *you. You* are the stock to pick.

It's time to invest in ourselves, to believe in ourselves. There will be some lessons along the way, but we can learn them and course-correct. Life is about wins and lessons, not wins and losses. As we learn, as we grow, as we find our way, we become better investors. We learn to minimize risk and maximize fulfillment. If we process our pain, we learn to love and give more of ourselves.

By investing in yourself, taking time for self-care, finding your hobby or art form, and listening to your intuition, you can unveil your vision. It is within you; it is a matter of remembrance. The noise and busyness of the world drown out what only you can know, your Soul Purpose. Your vision will become clear as you remove layers of misinformation, doubt, and scarcity. As you find time for yourself, you will find yourself. As you discover more about what you want, what you are capable of, and what inspires you, you can create your vision. Allow for your life and vision to evolve, to grow. Accept the vision, express it, live it, and then expand it. But don't allow consumerism or comparison to rob you of that vision. Materialism can persuade us to abandon our path in the name of expediency. If you don't take time for yourself, you will likely get stuck in the trap of living your life for someone else.

You don't have to know every step you must take to accomplish your vision—just know your win, then begin. Knowing all the steps would be impossible anyway, due to the disruptions of an ever-changing world. And besides, it could mean suffering the future. Suffering the future happens when you carry and dread the thought of what you have to do before you do it.

Suffering the future is exhausting. Instead, commit and then let the steps show up as you go along. Sometimes you have to invent them. Invention can be fun, but it can also be messy. Start with a blank slate rather than by copying or mimicking. What would you do if you knew you could not fail? What would you dedicate your time and energy to that means something to you? It is in the void that creation is possible. Remove fear, set censorship aside, and create.

**Suffering the Future**

*What happens when you carry and dread the thought of what you have to do before you do it.*

If your vision has never been realized before and requires invention, great. If you are enhancing what already exists, superb. Look at this from an angle of what engages you and how you want to create and play.

When you are just starting out or have not yet experienced what you consider success, consider that a gift; you have less baggage. If you have enjoyed some success and have some financial resources, you may be wrapped up in what you've already achieved and feel you have obligations that prevent you from creating your winning game. It is a normal part of the process to experience fear, doubt, and uncertainty. Use these emotions as indicators of what to address and find strategies for overcoming the constraint.

No matter where you are, determine if where you are going serves you. If you are running in the wrong direction, no amount of hard work will matter. Having the awareness to acknowledge that what you are doing is unfulfilling or unaligned with your Soul Purpose can be challenging. Putting more effort and money into a losing game may improve things financially, but does it get you where you want to go? It's hard to admit and address sunk costs. I've struggled with it. In 2007, I decided to design a software program to support my clients. At first this was exciting, but then it became expensive, confusing, and frustrating. I had invested $200,000 in the project, but I couldn't communicate well with the developers: it was like we didn't even speak the same language. The more they developed, the more confusing it became, and my team and clients had a hard time using the system. I spent another $100,000 before I finally killed that project—an extra $100,000 because I couldn't assess my sunk costs and tried to salvage something rather than deal in reality.

Where are you spending time and energy that is no longer serving you? What attachments do you have to projects, ideas, and people that drain your energy? These are sunk costs, too. Often, what seems like a great idea at first eventually infringes on your peace of mind, your life, and your flow. If you are on the wrong path or going the wrong way, moving further down the road won't get you any closer to what you really want.

Again, listen to your intuition. Invest time in your life and in yourself. Start with a blank sheet of paper and write down what you would do if money were of no concern. For me, it is comedy and combining comedy with finance. Follow your intuition and let go of your sunk costs. It is rarely convenient, but it is worth it.

The best thing you can invest in is creating your game. Invest time in your vision, in peers and mentors who can ask you great questions and call forward the best of who you are.

When I created the game called *Killing Sacred Cows,* I put everything into that book. Learning to write, edit, and design was an investment in myself. I knew nothing about publishing but hired a literary agent and book promoter so I could learn. These were investments that led to new skill sets and fed my purpose. Create meaningful work that is worthy of you, worthy of your life and time. Don't allow money, existing skills, or time to be an excuse. You can grow by delegating, collaborating, and finding co-creators. Your winning game will require that you allow other people to support you. That's how you invest in yourself: by engaging other people to make you better.

Lean into who you are because nobody else will. You are who you are, and nobody else in the world has the same combination of abilities. If you don't express what is within you, it dies. Nobody expects you to be perfect—and if they do, who cares? Choose expression over perfection. Listen to your intuition so you can live a life that's fulfilling to you.

In the next chapters, I'll share nine myths about money that keep you from building a life you love. It's easier to believe in these sacred cows when we are still driven by painful childhood memories. Now that you see the connection between the messages we carry forward from past experiences and our choices about money and business, you can shift money myths to truths that serve you and your financial destiny.

# Chapter Four

# Myth 1:
# The Finite Pie

IS THERE ONLY SO MUCH TO GO AROUND? IF ONE PERSON SUC-ceeds, is it at the expense of another? If resources are limited, how can everyone prosper? These questions have plagued civilization for centuries. They are the cause of much debate and divisiveness. Still, individuals' answers to these questions are predictable, based on perspective.

When people have a viewpoint rooted in the zero-sum, scarcity game, they believe there is only so much to go around. No amount of effort, savings, discipline, rate of return, luck, or advice from financial gurus can save you if you don't conquer this way of thinking. Scarcity brings out the worst in us. It is fed by a feeling of lack and reinforced by fear, pride, jealousy, selfishness, and adversarial competition. This is a mindset and becomes a way of being. Our ability or inability to shift from scarcity to abundance determines how we feel and treat others and informs the philosophy that leads to prosperity or destruction. Abundance helps us to increase our creativity, productivity, health, wealth, and happiness.

| MYTH: | REALITY: |
|---|---|
| *All resources are scarce and limited. If you want something for yourself, you'll have to take it from someone else.* | *There's enough for everyone, and we can always create more; we can prosper with others, not just at their expense.* |

For some, the statement "we can always create more" may seem reckless. In the context of destroying our environment due to a lack of stewardship and awareness, you are correct. That is not abundant, it is ignorant. Consumption at the expense of others or the earth is short-sighted and problematic. Win-lose follows the scarcity rule of take what you can, regardless of the effect.

Those who consider legacy in choices today move beyond immediate survival to create sustainability, adding wealth for generations to come. When we learn from each other, serve each other, and add value, we create wealth. This is true value. Value is not immediate gratification or competition at the expense of another, but a place where exchange makes both parties richer.

## THE PHILOSOPHY OF PROSPERITY

The first chapter of my book *Killing Sacred Cows,* "The Finite Pie," is about scarcity versus abundance. The notion of a finite pie means that if someone gets a piece, there's less for the next person. When we believe we're playing a zero-sum game, in which there's only so much to go around and we take at the expense of another, we get into a competitive mode; it's all about what we can get, even if that doesn't add value. The finite pie notion destroys people's prosperity because it isn't about giving the best of who they are. It isn't about adding value. It's simply a disease of the mind that leads to destruction and scarcity.

Clearly, money and pie aren't the same thing. The Federal Reserve adds to the money supply every minute. But even if there were a finite amount of money, it could change hands an infinite number of times. The more times money is exchanged, the more value is created. It's not as if there's only one pie and that pie will be gone someday. It's more like there is an infinite pie because people continue to bake more pies.

Even if we have finite resources, though, there is an infinite number of ways to be more resourceful, find new ways to produce value, and exchange with one another. Collaboration is the answer. Find the gift in differences. Celebrate and express your own abilities rather than wanting what someone else has.

> **Scarcity Mindset**
>
> *The belief that resources are limited and the world is a stage for a zero-sum game of accumulation. In scarcity, ownership by another means the loss of opportunity for oneself. When our actions are based on a scarcity mindset, we act on the fear that we won't get our fair share. This fear causes us to make irrational decisions, especially when it comes to our finances, that limit rather than enhance our potential.*

## SHIFTING OUT OF SCARCITY MINDSET

When I wrote "The Finite Pie," I knew that scarcity existed in our minds and that it could rule our lives. I knew the damage it could cause and the footprints of failure that could be traced back to it. But I didn't understand where scarcity came from. Now I know where these ideas begin and how to release their stranglehold. Scarcity comes from past experiences, especially childhood trauma. As I shared in Chapter Two, when we have unprocessed emotions or don't face our pain, scarcity remains. When we haven't healed from difficult situations or learned from past experiences, stress, pain, and avoidance limit our ability to be present, have peace, and live our best lives.

Often, we have a hard time remembering the most difficult times in our childhoods. Paradoxically, we hide the things that are most painful to avoid being hurt. Unfortunately, the very nature of hiding or running from these problems invites scarcity to run in the background and undermine our wealth and results. In these moments, we use escapism to avoid the pain. It is easy to complain and blame in these scenarios. Procrastination feeds scarcity and limits our power to create our vision, to live fulfilled lives.

Scarcity exists due to skewed philosophies, false beliefs. Sometimes those beliefs are rooted in our childhood trauma, and sometimes they are handed down from other people and society. Ask yourself about the messages you heard growing up. What did friends, family members, teachers, and preachers say about people with money? At what point did you see people behave in a detrimental way, chasing money? Where were you judged positively or negatively around money?

It can be difficult to let go of entrenched beliefs around money. If you grew up in poverty, or if that mindset is part of your family culture, learning about people who have overcome their limitations—including limited thinking—can help you shift your mindset. Just seeing what is possible can retrain your brain.

When I was fifteen, I started interviewing successful people in my community. I knew they had a different perspective than my family did, and I wanted to understand it. In high school, I joined programs and built relationships with teachers who spent time with me outside the classroom. One of those teachers, Teri Tubbs, sponsored me for Students in Free Enterprise competitions. This helped me begin to develop skills in communication and business building and gave me a glimpse of the promise of entrepreneurship. I participated in the Governor's Honors Academy, a summer program where I met senators, inventors, and other bright students. I remember meeting Renn Zaphiropolous, who invented Xerox technology, and that he taught us about cooking and compared it to business. He taught the concept of using basic elements to create consistent results in cooking (heat and timing were essential) and that you could experiment to expand on recipes and create new ones. He then introduced us to his basic recipe for profit in business, which I used in the car detailing business I had started the year before. My income quadrupled. Then I took part of the profit and invested it back into the business. Renn's core message was about developing skills and investing in people and relationships. What I remember best is that he made me feel like success was within reach if I was willing to learn and apply his message.

After my interaction with Renn, I gained confidence and started to approach other successful people and ask great questions. You might be surprised by how willing people are to help when you ask them for guidance in earnest. Find out what they value and how you might be able to support them, or simply acknowledge how they have impacted you. Create value first, then make deposits in Relationship Capital.

> ### Abundance Mindset
>
> *The belief that there are more than enough resources to fulfill the desires of all people within a society. At the heart of abundance is a belief in human ingenuity and human value, and a dedication to applying as much of your own value and ingenuity as you can to the improvement of your life and society.*

The best way to move out of scarcity is to be in service. Find more ways to serve people. Use your Relationship and Mental Capital to help others. The more you do this, the more entrenched your abundance mindset will become.

## WE WERE BORN TO BE CREATORS

The finite pie belief that a win for one is at the expense of another leads to anger and isolation. This belief system, a sacred cow, prevents cooperation. Wealth begins within, with our gifts, talents, and abilities, and is a function of our perspective. Exchange creates wealth. When we add value through serving others and solving problems, money is the by-product.

In today's world, technology has brought forth new possibilities at minimal cost that would have required millions of dollars in the past. Through open source, blockchain, and other innovations, we can accomplish more with less money, in less time, and with less complication. Innovation comes from a perspective of abundance and collaboration. When I wrote *Killing Sacred Cows,* technology was in its infancy compared to what it is capable of today. What might have seemed impossible then now seems inevitable. Through crowdsourcing, new companies succeed at an unprecedented rate. Access to capital comes from clients rather than borrowed funds or forfeited equity. This is an amazing collaboration, funded by the end user rather than a bank or the vultures of venture capital. You might be one idea or one relationship away from removing a major obstacle, from realizing momentum with any idea or project.

We live in a time of unprecedented wealth. Yet due to the persistence of the old paradigm that tells us to take at the expense of others, there is still another level of wealth we can achieve together. This begins when we abolish the sacred cow of the finite pie by enlisting others' support, living our purpose, and adding value through serving others.

We were born to be creators and to make our lives extraordinary with the gifts we're given. By becoming consciously aware of our own natures, we can begin to let go of scarcity and fear and begin to accept and express abundance. As we begin to think abundantly, the changes in our thoughts and behavior manifest externally. As James Allen wrote in his book *As a Man Thinketh,* "Men do not attract that which they want, but that which they are."[3]

# Chapter Five

# Myth 2:
# Money Is Power

ONEY CAN HELP US ACCESS RESOURCES, BUY CONVE-
nience, hire people, and bring attention (wanted or unwanted).
This can seem like power, but money is merely a receipt of
stored value, a by-product of value. Money doesn't have inherent power; it is
merely a concept. But when money is misunderstood, people feel powerless
(or powerful). This is evident if we examine how people act in the pursuit
of money, the allure of a falsehood that is temporary at best. You know the
lie that artificially props up money: more is better, sexier; money makes you
more valuable, more appreciated, and of higher worth as person. This is
even reflected in the terms we use to measure and describe money, like "net
worth," "appreciation," and "value."

Money can be efficient. It can be extraordinarily useful. But without vision, without your winning game, more money can mean more
distraction.

Again, money is an idea, a concept, and it is massively misunderstood.
Take the adage "Money is the root of all evil," for example. It has become a
belief for many people, and they make decisions based on this belief. This
belief is not just a myth; the phrase is also taken out of context and only
part of the original statement. The correct wording, which comes from
the Bible, is "love of money is the root of all evil."[4] Money has no power
except the power that people give it. Love of money—over people—can
be powerful and cause people to do "evil" things, but money itself is not
evil. Money is an effect, or a by-product; value creation is the cause.

I believe that prosperity and Soul Purpose are synonymous. We feel fulfilled when serving others if our service is consistent with our Soul Purpose. The more we do this, the more we prosper. Using this empowering definition of prosperity defeats the myth that money is the root of all evil, because we can't prosper unless we help people.

| MYTH: *Money is power. Therefore, money is evil.* | REALITY: *Money is nothing more than an expression and by-product of value created by people.* |
|---|---|

## WHEN WE BELIEVE THAT MONEY IS POWER

When we believe that money is power, we relinquish control to external forces (corporations, government, or luck) and limit our ability to act in the moment. We lose our power and chase money at the expense of our lives, our happiness. This justifies our sacrifice of what is most important in order to earn, to build net worth. Thinking that money is power can also cause good people to do things in the name of money that aren't in the best interest of others. We justify our actions based upon a system that seemingly rewards takers, but this is never sustainable. When we link our own value with the amount of money we have, money has power over us—money, an inanimate object, a piece of paper printed in a certain way or digits on a computer screen.

When we think that money is power, our actions become predictable. We hustle, grind, work, and deprioritize everything else: our health, our families, our dreams. Our false belief in money's power takes hold, giving our own power over to the hope of an impossible future. We are at the service of the next dollar and the next opportunity, slaves to false promise of more money—more significance, more happiness, more, more, more.

When we choose to make a buck at any cost, we compromise the best of who we are and those who love us the most.

Although money may give us access to resources like labor, materials, and even time, money alone cannot solve problems or replace human ingenuity and innovation. It is through Soul Purpose, and tapping into our Mental and Relationship Capital, that we can find our power and therefore add value, serve others, and solve problems.

If money can solve the problem, it isn't really a problem. Throwing money at problems won't create solutions for some of the biggest problems we face. In the US, we have spent massive amounts of money to try to address health, including mental health, addiction, and homelessness. There is more money spent in the United States on hospitals, doctors, medications, and all things health than in any other country, and yet we are not the healthiest country—far from it.

Money without responsibility is a path to destruction. Money without Soul Purpose is a recipe for unlimited desire and demand, and a lack of fulfillment.

## CURRENCY

When it comes to money, it is how we utilize it that matters, not how much of it we collect. Think of it like the current that goes through speaker wire to bring sound from the amplifier to the speaker. Collecting speaker wire isn't the answer; it is the current that matters. Amassing net worth is similar to amassing speaker wire. Unless there is a way for it to flow (sound or cash flow), it is relatively useless. With money, the utility we truly seek is connection.

Without a feeling of connection to our Soul Purpose or to other people in relationship, we feel alone. Isolation is fuel for worry and despair. Money alone cannot solve this; it is merely a tool that can help us access the production of other people in the form of goods and services. But what good is money if it is not utilized or shared? If you could have all the money in the world, but with the caveat that you had to be alone, would it be worth it? Of course not.

There is an irrational fear around money because we have been told it changes people and that more money will change us. Many people fear wealth because they think the change will be for the worse, and still others invite wealth because they think that it will make them happy. The amount of currency available to you makes you more of what you already are. If you are naturally generous, increased wealth will simply give you greater opportunity to be generous. If you are greedy, wealth will do nothing but manifest your greed even more clearly. A bank balance alone does not have the power to change people; only people can change their understanding of and relationship with their bank balance. If you're unhappy without money, you'll never be happy with it. Money is important and useful, but if you think that money will fix your problems, that thought is the problem.

Power comes from connection—being connected to our Soul Purpose, connected to relationships. People are the only true assets, and our relationship to others is powerful.

When we believe that money is the obstacle, or that if we only had more, everything would be okay, we limit our ability to learn, ignore the root of our issue, diminish our resourcefulness, and lose sight of people and value in the name of a receipt.

Again, money is a receipt. We use it to store value. It is a receipt that can be redeemed to tap into the value of others, but if we don't know what we want or what matters to us, money can never be a worthy substitute. When we have a vision, money can support that vison. When we know our value, money can help us to get support in growing that value.

## THE BY-PRODUCT OF VALUE

When we look at money as a by-product of value, rather than as a signifier of luck or a tool of greed, it informs our actions so that they are aligned with prosperity and abundance. There are plenty of businesses and investments that provide little for society and reduce value at the expense of others. Flash trading—using supercomputers to skim money off of trades—is a great example. There are plenty of tools created by Wall Street designed with win-lose in mind. Anytime you run into a something-for-nothing proposition, be cautious. Choose value, as it leads to a more fulfilling life.

Another example of making money with little value is day trading. Day trading provides no value to society. Day traders use options, bets with winners and losers. Simply clicking a mouse doesn't provide value for both parties.

Once, when my wife and I were at a writing event, we got to talking with the woman sitting next to us. She told us that she was writing a book on day trading.

I asked, "What value does that provide?"

"I can live anywhere."

"No, no. I get the value it provides for you," I said. "What value does it provide for the world?"

She didn't have an answer.

Sometimes we think that if we made money, we must have created value. Yet esoteric things like derivatives simply mean that the rich get richer by taking money from hardworking people who set their money aside for the American dream, believing that one day, someday, their portfolios will perform for them. Most of the time, they find out this was not the case because of too many fees, too many losses due to too much risk, and too much skimming and volatility.

My grandfather didn't have a lot of money, but he was wealthy within our family because we loved and adored him. If he had taken all that value and given it to the world, he probably would have had much more wealth, but that wasn't his objective. His objective was to love and support his family. Some will say that if you're not successful in the world, you're not successful at all, but others define success as being loved and adored by their families.

It's not a question of either-or. You can be there for both your family and the world if you establish your win, create your rules, and know your parameters. If you don't, the world will create the rules for you, and it won't reward you for a good family life or a great marriage.

If we think of assets in the context of adding value for people, we understand the secret of investing. The greater the number of people who are impacted by something, or the greater the impact on those people, the more profitable that thing will be. Profit exists as a by-product of value to people.

## FINANCIAL FREEDOM

Many people think that their ultimate goal is financial freedom. Some think financial freedom is an amount of money in the bank or the time when they can finally retire. I think of it as a state of mind in which money is no longer the primary reason to do or not do something. Money is still *a* consideration; it's not *the* primary consideration.

When you have financial freedom, money is no longer your reason or excuse for doing or not doing something, so it doesn't have power over you.

Price, cost, and value are all factors in financial freedom. When people are only focused on price, they are never financially free. They buy something for 40% off retail, but were they going to buy it anyway?

Then there is cost: the economic impact. Some things are low-price, high-cost. I once flew Frontier Airlines. Okay, it wasn't that bad, but the seat didn't move back and I'm pretty tall. But the real reason it was low-price, high-cost was that I couldn't use my laptop, which meant I couldn't work.

Processed food is another example of low-price, high-cost. You buy it at the dollar store to save money, but it's made with high-fructose corn syrup. That's going to be low-price and high-cost if it leads to diabetes or other health problems.

Given the alternative, I would much rather have a high-priced, low-cost accountant. Some accountants are super cheap, but they're historians: "Here's what you made. Here's what you owe." They aren't looking to the future and providing value by strategizing how to lower taxes. Low-price, high-cost, because you just paid twice as much tax as was required.

Value is your overall sense of satisfaction and fulfillment. It is also a personal preference, in the eye of the beholder. Financial freedom has to do with thinking value first, cost second, and price third. When we think about price and price alone, we're not financially free at all. I'm willing to spend more on first-class airfare because I can get a lot of writing done on a flight; it's productive for me. This makes me more money than I would save by flying coach.

Some people in the play-not-to-lose scarcity mindset spend so much time saving that they lose sight of the big picture. When I was first married, I was still living in a scarcity mindset.

I remember my wife asking, "Why don't we have cable anymore?"

"I'm saving money," I said.

"Why is it so hot in here?"

"I turned down the air-conditioning."

Every decision I made was about saving money.

Again, financial freedom is when money is no longer your primary reason for doing or not doing something. I remember that, during those early years, it was hard to enjoy much of anything. If it didn't provide income, I didn't want to do it. I worked hard during that time of my life, but it didn't lead to the best results because I was laboring without vision. I was too busy working and saving. This limited the money and time I invested in myself. It was hard to have a retreat for a couple of days because it did not provide direct income. I thought, *If I'm not meeting clients, I'm not making money.*

Eventually, my business partners encouraged me to take the extra time I was spending budgeting, cutting back, and worrying about costs and use it differently. They locked me in the office on a Saturday to spend ten hours focusing on what I could do to improve my production, what I could do to add more value. It was hard, but that was when I came up with an idea to start a study group for financial professionals. It started with a small group that met once a month in our office. Eventually, we were regularly filling a hotel amphitheater, doing weekly conference calls, and creating enough recurring revenue to cover my basic expenses. Ten hours of thinking created a game of production rather than reduction, leading to more fulfillment and more money.

## QUALITY OF LIFE AND LEGACY

The best of the wealthy focus on quality of life and legacy. Some don't; some are addicted, greedy bastards who just want to make more at any cost and crush everyone along the way. These people are the reason we still believe that money is power and "the root of all evil." We hear about them in the news, but don't hear nearly enough about the good people who really care, who do good and are always looking for more ways to do good. These people want to help others heal and pay it forward to impact society. There are many of them, but they're not saying, "Hey, look at me and how great I am." They just do what they do because it's who they are.

In recent years, I have met some billionaires and become friends with a handful of them. Contrary to the media narrative, they are some of the best people you will ever meet. They're consistently thinking, *How can I support? How can I help? What can I do?* They invest in their families, and they think about legacy.

I am writing this book because of my desire to help restore people's faith and hope in humanity. I want to help people get their finances in order so they can start thinking more productively about their purpose and their impact on the people who matter most to them. When we're overly stressed about our finances, we become frustrated, we don't think logically, and we're not present. We don't have time to heal our childhood trauma, go out into nature, or take up a hobby. All of that robs from our quality of life, and the key to real wealth is quality of life.

Do we have quality of life, or is it just quantity of stuff? We all know deep down that the joy of possession is only temporary. Temporary happiness—is that really happiness? I could feel good buying something and then, two weeks later, forget that I ever bought it.

It really comes down to quality of life and quality of relationships. If we have quality relationships with ourselves and other people in our lives, that's true wealth.

Can a person who has little material property be happy? Yes, assuming that she has quality relationships and is on a path of discovering and living her Soul Purpose. Can a person with a relatively large amount of money be happy? Yes, again assuming that he has quality relationships and is using his material wealth to find and live his Soul Purpose. Neither our happiness nor our misery depends on the amount of money we possess. There are miserable people with money and miserable people without money. Happiness is about fulfillment, which means you won't always be happy in every moment. Things can make you temporarily happy that don't necessarily offer long-term fulfillment. So be careful about making choices for momentary happiness at the expense of living your Soul Purpose.

Bringing a vision to fruition takes work—work like dealing with our childhood issues, facing insecurities, and breaking through frustration to find our value. If we're not aligned with our Soul Purpose, we're not prospering.

Feeling fulfilled is the single best indicator of our level of abundance. Prosperity brings fulfillment and fulfillment brings prosperity. You can't have one without the other.

If we pursue our potential to be prosperous, we create maximum value for ourselves and other people. Allowing the myth that money is power to influence whether and how we achieve wealth limits our potential. We must keep in mind that the opportunities for us to create value for others and ourselves are endless, limited only by our misconceptions.

## Chapter Six

# Myth 3:
# It's All About the Numbers

W HEN YOU SEARCH A NOTABLE PERSON'S NAME ON THE web, you'll almost always see "net worth" come up as an additional search term. Net worth. The numbers. How much they are "worth" after liabilities. We equate worth with the numbers, not the person.

Prosperity has less to do with our financial numbers on paper and more to do with our happiness and fulfillment. This shift in mindset helps us to put numbers in their proper perspective.

| MYTH: *Wealth means numbers on account balances, and you'd better hope they're big numbers.* | REALITY: *Wealth is building a life you love, finding joy and fulfillment. Focusing primarily on numbers often prevents the achievement of true wealth.* |
| --- | --- |

## NUMBERS DON'T TELL THE WHOLE STORY

Numbers are a great tool for measuring what can be measured, but what matters most often cannot be measured.

What is the monetary value of a kiss, a compliment, or a hug?

What is the monetary value of a nap?

How much is it worth to write a joke and perform onstage for the first time, facing fears and feeling the elation of seeing a thought in one's mind create connection in the crowd?

Some of my best memories are of moments that didn't require money. In others, money was a helpful companion. Money has allowed me to travel, eat at great restaurants, and stay at nice hotels, but during my first year of college, for example, I didn't have much money. I did have plenty of fun and create lots of great memories.

I'll always remember our family retreat on December 5th, 2020. My parents, sister, brother-in-law, and wife all joined with some facilitators to spend a transformational day together. As we talked about being open with each other—and our commitment not to succumb to worry or a tendency to isolate, but to pick up the phone or make the drive to connect instead—we agreed that we could rely on each other. Talk to each other. Be there for each other.

We were rewriting how to be a family. How to connect.

In the past, the pattern was worrying and staying silent. My mom had nearly died before her kidney transplant, and my parents kept it from us because they didn't want to worry us. In my family, we were taught to keep quiet about things rather than share them. But on this day, we shared. We had tough conversations. We talked about things that we had held in for years. Can the value of this be measured in dollars?

What is the value of forgiveness and connection? What would you trade every dollar to have back or do differently? Life doesn't work that way. It is filled with lessons, memories, and people. How do you quantify life or reduce it to a number? You don't.

I remember holding my dad's hand and looking into my mom's eyes during our family retreat. I felt love. I felt connection. Telling them how much they mean to me and how much I love them felt amazing. They were able to tell my wife how generous they think she is and how she truly is family. What is the cost of a conversation?

See, there is no price for entry to our family functions, where we laugh so hard it hurts. When my son had some major health challenges, my parents let us know that we weren't alone, and that they would do whatever it would take. The feeling that created has nothing to do with numbers.

It isn't all about the numbers. Nah, it's all about the connection. It's all about love. It's all about Soul Purpose.

Money is helpful. Useful. Efficient. But life isn't measured in numbers so much as moments and memories.

## YOUR PORTFOLIO OF VALUES

A friend asked me, "I've got some money invested. Would you take a look at my portfolio?"

I said, "I'm no longer an investment advisor. I can't give you any investment advice, but I can give you some philosophical notes. I know you pretty well. When I look at the stocks you hold, some of them don't add up to who you are. You own Lockheed Martin, but you don't seem like a missile guy. You own Philip Morris; I don't think you're into smoking. Invest in alignment with your Soul Purpose. You'll be more informed and more connected to the outcomes."

We vote with our dollars. I don't invest in the stock market because I don't love Wall Street as it is now. Originally, it was a way for companies to raise capital to build infrastructure. Now, it is often a way for people to take money from other people and exit. It is riddled with wrongdoing and a lack of accountability. We see this with companies that attracted a massive amount of money even before they went public, like WeWork. These funds inflated the value of the company; the CEO of WeWork even cashed out $700 million before it was profitable. There were plenty of funds, but without a viable financial model. Media buzz generated an abundance of attention and drove up the potential value before the initial public offering (IPO), but it was an overvalued IPO. There was a big difference between the amount of capital WeWork received and their ability to create profit. Who eventually got screwed? The investors, not the owners. The owners were able to live an extraordinary lifestyle, while the investors were left with something very different than it was supposed to be.

This is why I have a problem with the stock market. Private companies and small businesses employ more people overall than big businesses do. They're doing plenty of good. Contrast that with the cronyism and corruption of some major corporations that get bailed out by the government and don't seem to care about people or the environment. They don't even care to tell the truth, because they need the shareholder value to go up. They want to squash innovation so that they can continue to reign.

I've opted out of the system, and my life is better. My emotions don't go up and down along with the market. I invest in what I know, what I enjoy, and areas that enhance my lifestyle today and will in the future. This is my Investor DNA.

Investor DNA is how we relate to investment. Most retirement planners are only selling funds. This has nothing to do with a client's Investor DNA.

## INVESTOR DNA

Let's explore the idea of Investor DNA a little further, using the analogy of genetics. At one point, it was believed that your genetics created your destiny. Then a newer field called epigenetics emerged, which showed that your DNA only determines 2–10% of who you are; epigenetics unlocks or activates the rest.

Your Investor DNA means that certain things come more naturally to you, and you can continue to learn and develop.

The first part of your Investor DNA is your set of *core values,* your script for how to operate. Corporations spell out their company values; unfortunately, most individuals do not. When we value something, we treat it differently than something we don't care as much about.

Then we look at our *core drivers*. We ask not only what is valuable to us, but what we are passionate about.

Then we add in our *core competencies*. What do we have the ability to learn at an accelerated rate because it is part of our best skill set? What do we, because of who we are, understand more quickly than others do?

CORE VALUES + CORE DRIVERS + CORE COMPETENCIES = INVESTOR DNA

I am someone with financial competency. I can study and remember its lingo with interest and ease where, to other people, it is a foreign language. I can dissect a 401(k) and understand its pros and cons, what works and doesn't work. I understand money as a concept, so I can see beyond the numbers of a spreadsheet, which is what most people think money is about. This competency is part of my Investor DNA.

Investor DNA is taking that competency and using it to learn at an accelerated rate. It's what we're excited about because it drives us and is valuable to us. It's who we are.

When we are aware of our Investor DNA, we can relate those qualities to the investments we make. When Facebook issued its IPO, people offered me the opportunity to purchase some Facebook stock. But it didn't fit my core values. I thought, *I don't love Facebook. I don't know a lot about it. It's not part of my Investor DNA.* Some of those people made a lot of money on it and told me how much I could have made. I say I could have gotten distracted.

This is the key distinction. Without knowing their Investor DNA, most people cannot discern between an opportunity and a distraction.

## OPPORTUNITIES AND DISTRACTIONS

Here's an example of a distraction that felt like an opportunity. My brother-in-law once came to me and said, "I'm going to close on this property. I need $25,000 to put it in escrow. I already have a buyer; I just need to get it under contract. I'll give you back $50,000 within three months." I agreed to the deal, and he did exactly as he said he would. Annualized, that's a 400% return.

You might qualify that investment as an opportunity. It wasn't. Did I know what it took to find that property, fix it up, or find the buyer? No. It felt like an opportunity because of the Relationship Capital I had. But it gave me a false sense of personal achievement. I confused being lucky with being good.

Another friend told me about a real estate deal that netted $190,000, half of which I got. Again, lucky, not good. With no knowledge of the industry, I made a ton of money on my first four or five real estate deals.

In fact, by 2007, I owned over one hundred properties without having much real estate knowledge. Then 2008 came and, as Warren Buffett says, "Only when the tide goes out do you discover who's been swimming naked."[5] All ships rise with the rising tide. When it rolls back, you find out who really knows what they're doing.

I didn't know many real estate strategies, so I had to learn them. It took up more than 50% of my time, which meant my business suffered in 2008. It was my first down year because I was distracted by what I had thought was an opportunity. Because it was not aligned with my Investor DNA, it ended up costing me time and money.

I invested in my cabin because I know the area and I love and utilize the cabin. It is my sanctuary for rejuvenation and content creation and the headquarters for one of my businesses, and has a podcast studio and room for immersions with clients. I invest in my businesses. Creating intellectual property, like my books and my comedy special, is part of my Investor DNA. It's who I am and I'm passionate about it.

Most people think of investment as stocks, bonds, and real estate. I think of investments as books, places, and skill sets because that's who I am. Who are you? Are you investing in things that you value and understand?

## WINS AND LESSONS

I once owned property in Franklin, Tennessee, that I'd never even seen. My partner went bankrupt, and I had made a personal guarantee, which meant that I couldn't just walk away from the property and give it to the bank; they had attachments to my assets.

I had to make seven trips to Tennessee to deal with this situation. It was a huge stress. I had made the investment based upon the idea that my partner had the knowledge and I had the money. Handling the negative cash flow created strain and stress. At one point, the negative cash flow from all of my properties led me to borrow money to pay for my son's speech therapy. This caused me pain, stress, and a feeling of failure. I ended up paying the most expensive tuition: experience. When I finally finished handling this investment, I wondered, *What questions should*

*I have asked before investing, knowing what I know now?* That painful moment started to unveil the concept of Investor DNA.

I realized that risk is in the investor, not the investment.

How can two different people own similar properties, but one makes money while the other loses money? Well, one owner might understand strategies like fractionalized ownership, Airbnb arbitrage, and seller financing, or have a list of potential buyers.

I've interviewed investor Robert Kiyosaki several times over the years. He loves real estate and still attends real estate seminars. He treats it like a business.

At one point I told him, "You have a list of millions of people, all interested in buying real estate. Real estate is different for you than for someone who doesn't have those connections. You have more Investor DNA."

From 2002 to 2006, property in Las Vegas, Nevada went up in value. You actually had to enter a lottery to buy some new homes because there was such demand, but much of the demand was artificial. Investors were buying and squatting, thinking, *Six months from now, I'm going to sell this for a $100,000 gain.* Nobody was thinking in terms of Investor DNA, and nobody realized that people are the asset; they thought that property was the asset. Eventually, too many investors were buying homes. This flooded the rental market with brand-new properties whose rents were a fraction of the monthly expense of a mortgage, and the market came crashing down.

A large portion of Wealth Factory clients specialize in the field of health. Some are at the forefront of the latest studies and advancements, and are writing books and publishing research on the topic. They know the people behind the companies and breakthroughs. One of these clients followed CBD companies in Canada, as he thought that cannabis would soon be legalized there. He was in the conversations, knew the people involved, and knew what was happening, giving him an advantage with his Investor DNA. The returns were spectacular.

I have another good friend and client named Mike. He came to one of our Wealth Factory workshops and learned about Investor DNA. At the time, he had money in mutual funds. After learning about Investor DNA, he called his broker and said, "Let's get rid of all my mutual funds and invest in things I know. I love Tesla, I drive a Tesla, and I'm likely to buy another. Let's invest in Tesla." He thought of other things he used daily or companies that made his life better. He invested money there instead, with massive success.

Mike went on to invest in other companies he understood. He bought ten companies over the next several years and was up over 100% on the entire portfolio over a fifteen-month period when the market was flat.

There's a risk or downside that requires a word of caution. Just because we love something doesn't mean it's going to work. We can buy on emotion because we want something to work, not because it has the fundamentals. The key is to establish a team that helps us, with due diligence, to see the things that we may not otherwise see.

## AUTHENTIC PROSPERITY

Most—if not all—of us want to prosper, but do we even have a clear definition of what prosperity actually is? Is it an amount of money? Is it retirement? I submit that to prosper means that we are fulfilled because we're doing what we were born to do. It's that simple: if people are truly, deeply fulfilled, then they prosper regardless of the amount of money they have in that moment. Again, I want to emphasize that being fulfilled doesn't mean always being happy. Being uncomfortable is part of learning and growing. Doing hard things so you can develop skill sets or implement an idea will not always make you happy in the moment, but you will be engaged in work that is worth doing. There are ebbs and flows in life. If you know your Soul Purpose and your win, fulfillment is inevitable.

If your primary measure of success is the amount of money you make, remember, someone else will always make more. Equating money with success can lead to more money, but it can also override fulfillment, drain energy, and feel empty. Contrary to the myth, prosperity is a function of feeling fulfilled and connected and enjoying a high quality of life, not a function of numbers. We can have a lot of money and still be miserable. We can have no money and be miserable. We can also have a lot of money and be happy or have no money and be happy. The point is to stop focusing on money and start focusing on fulfillment, knowing your win, and living your Soul Purpose. Since fulfillment cannot be quantified, it's ridiculous to base our happiness on hypothetical, magical future numbers. If we focus on ourselves first, on knowing our win and our value and delivering that value, the money we require will naturally follow.

If you want to prosper, find out what it is that will truly make you feel fulfilled. Seek, find, and live your Soul Purpose. Focus on the cause of money—creating value for others—and let the effect naturally follow.

## Chapter Seven

# Myth 4:
# The Long Haul

H AVE YOU EVER HEARD SOMEONE SAY, "FOR THE LONG haul" and thought that sounded exciting? Hardly. It sounds more like a reason to give condolences. You don't want to get call from your dentist or mechanic saying you are in it for the long haul, so why would you want to hear that from a retirement planner?

**Accumulation Theory**

*The financial theory that emphasizes building a large enough sum of money to live off the interest and never touch the principal. Common accumulation products include 401(k)s, IRAs and other qualified plans, and mutual funds. In the accumulation theory, net worth is the greatest indicator of wealth. The theory tends toward scarcity in that those who practice it develop the scarcity mindset through years of frugal saving, often in fear of losing their accumulated money.*

The accumulation theory limits wealth and requires people to believe three things:

1. It takes money to make money;
2. High risk equals high return; and
3. You are in it for the long haul.

Accumulation theory centers on the belief that the amount of money you invest plus the amount of risk you take—combined with the amount of time you are willing to wait—are the keys to future wealth. All three of these tenets of the accumulation theory are dangerous in today's disruptive economy. Accumulation theory teaches us to set it and forget it and invest early and often, and always so you can compound interest for long periods of time.

An alternative would be to accelerate your wealth by focusing on cash flow.

Accumulation is more dangerous now than ever before. Technology invites and accelerates change. For example, we now see smaller, more adaptable companies displacing large ones at an increased rate. This will negatively impact the overall return for index and mutual funds and cause a higher rate of bankruptcy among previously stable companies and industries.

The advice in retirement planning has been to compound interest so you will have a nest egg to live off of in thirty years. But in today's low interest rate environment, the cash flow from a nest egg is diminished. Creating predictable cash flow using fixed income instruments promoted by retirement planners (like bonds, CDs, money market accounts, fixed annuities, and the like) requires much larger sums of money to produce a decent lifestyle. Retirement planners are less likely to teach you about Decentralized Finance (DeFi; more on that in Chapter Thirteen) or other options because there is no compensation model for them. Basically, where can you create cash flow from your assets without losing principal or sleep?

| MYTH: | REALITY: |
|---|---|
| *Put all your money in a 401(k) and forget about it. Retirement is going to cost you everything you can possibly save and maybe a little more.* | *Don't let your money stagnate beyond your control. Use it immediately so it can benefit you now and in the future.* |

## HOARDING

When people hoard—amass things and hold on to them without utilizing them—they don't get true value from what they have. If we hoard our money, it becomes stagnant and we limit the value it can provide for us.

Some people are poisoned by the belief that they need to scrimp, save, sacrifice, defer, and delay so that someday they can finally retire. They believe that when they have a nest egg, they'll get to live off the measly bit of interest it generates (which, most of the time, is all taxable). They plod through lives that they don't really love or enjoy so that one day they can have this so-called dream; meanwhile, they also become vulnerable to fluctuating interest rates, taxes, and inflation, which rob them of purchasing power. Again, when interest rates are low, as they have been for a long time now, retired people suffer—even more if taxes rise.

With an almost 40% increase in the money supply due to a concept called "quantitative easing," the Federal Reserve has watered down the soup by making our money less valuable. Adding such an exorbitant amount of money without value creation, labor, or exchange has created inflation, decimating our purchasing power. Those on a fixed income have been hurt and had to make tough choices about what to do. Many have had to tap into savings, use credit cards, or simply cut out enjoyment—and in many cases necessities—just to live.

The people who believe that there's only so much to go around and that one day they can finally live on their interest are finding that they're not living the lives they were told they could, and that the size of the nest egg required to provide their desired lifestyle is a moving target outside of their influence or control. They are told what rate of interest will be paid by institutions, or how much they owe in tax by their government, and are witnessing rapid increases in the prices of food, utilities, and other basic amenities. The sacred cows of the past have been disrupted by inflation. They are being exposed.

So now the question for us to answer is: what can you do about it? Begin by taking back control of your finances and taking responsibility for your life.

We've been told to budget and save 10% of our income. Well, that 10% that was supposed to be saved is now being used to buy the same things that were 10% lower in price just a few years ago. Budgeting isn't the answer. Taking more risk isn't the answer. Using the long haul system, well, unfortunately, hasn't worked as well as advertised.

When we shirk responsibility, money is elusive, confusing, and feels like a matter of luck when it comes to our investments. We work to provide a lifestyle. Then we hope that we'll be able to retire because we're exhausted from all the sacrifice required to provide that lifestyle. But at retirement, we're rewarded with uncertainty instead of freedom. Again, those in retirement are concerned that all the sacrifice and saving has not provided what was promised because interest rates are so low, inflation is so high, and the threat of rising taxes is very real.

With the long haul approach, we remove accountability along the way. If the market goes down, we think we have more time. Mountain charts presented by mutual funds show exponential returns in the last few years before retirement, but what if the market doesn't get the message and money is lost instead? This is putting our lives in the hands of Wall Street and the government, trying to navigate the future and predict how much we will need without knowing what our lives or the world will be like thirty years from today.

Instead, live by the code of value creation because the by-product is more wealth. Invest in your ability to create and deliver value. Invest in yourself first, foremost, and always. Focus on ways to increase your cash flow rather than how to accumulate money for thirty years. Net worth is relatively worthless if it can't create cash flow or sustain your lifestyle in retirement.

## WALL STREET PROMISES

People are tired, bitter, and even angry because they're chasing a retirement plan dream that doesn't exist. They're told to sacrifice now for a better future and end up doing things they don't enjoy today in hopes of a better tomorrow. Working hard, trading time for money, and choosing a career or job that provides minimal fulfillment are big reasons why they don't have the commitment to handling their finances and leave them to the promises of Wall Street. The exhaustion makes it feel like they hardly have the energy or the time.

Would you trust Wall Street if it was any other business? Wall Street airlines: "We'll get you there 87% of the time." Wall Street hospital: "Was the surgery a success? Well, it was for Wall Street; they got paid."

We know that we wouldn't trust Wall Street in those situations, but somehow we think it's our only investment option because they've convinced us that money is too complicated for us: we're not to be trusted with our money, but they are. Yet look at the scandals. Goldman Sachs nearly destroyed Malaysia, but nobody went to jail.

We feel limited in our options if we are intimidated by finance. By merely trusting our advisors without understanding our investments and just hoping, not knowing, we increase our risk.

In the retirement planning long haul model, we don't co-create or collaborate. We are told what to do via jargon from the financial industry and hope and trust that they know what is best. We have been taught, trained, and educated to say, "Please take care of my money. I don't have the energy for it, and you are the expert."

And with that, you've just given a piece of who you are for a hope and a plan that has no capacity to deliver. Is your planner actually trading the portfolio, or are they handing it to another portfolio manager? Does your planner know your Investor DNA, how to create cash flow today, and how to help you keep more of what you make without budgeting?

Or is your planner still citing the 10% average in the market that was fueled by dot-com boom of the nineties? Remember the dot-com/dot-bomb? How many of those companies are here today? Very few. We are in a similar bubble now, but with cryptocurrency. There is plenty of hype and plenty of returns, but there will be plenty of losses as well.

The most dangerous part of the long haul is when we fund retirement plans before we invest in ourselves. The long haul preaches the importance of starting early because of the time value of money. Start early, or it will cost you.

Now any dollar you spend on yourself is competing with your retirement and future net worth. A budgeting mindset can create dollars to fund future plans at the expense of immediate skill sets. There are people funding retirement plans while paying double-digit interest rates on credit cards, or putting money into plans that earn less than they pay in interest. This is the mindset that comes along with the long haul. The societal messages that create this mindset are dogmatic and deliberate, and the approach can be at odds with your Soul Purpose.

I want to reinforce this point: you are your greatest asset. How can you grow as a person? What skill sets would allow you to make more money and feel more fulfilled? What would create a better outcome: one more deposit in a retirement account, or healing childhood wounds and trauma? What investment would be more rewarding: learning a skill that leads to making more money for years, or making another deposit that you won't touch until age sixty-five or later?

I am so passionate about this concept, this topic, and helping people defeat this myth that in 2008, I created a challenge called "The 401(k) Hoax." I took on one hundred *Killing Sacred Cows* readers as one-on-one clients and committed to doubling the return on the money they invested in personal coaching with me. At the end of the year, we would compare the return on the same amount of money in their retirement plan. I gave them a guarantee that, if they didn't add at least twice the amount of cash to their bottom line, I would not only give them their money back, I would also double the return they would have received from their 401(k)s during that period out of my own pocket. Ninety-seven of the one hundred clients worked with me for the entire process. We employed tax savings strategies, restructured loans, negotiated better interest rates, and redesigned insurance plans to put more money in their pockets, far exceeding the performance of any mutual fund. Then we took some of the savings and had them invest in themselves by taking courses in their fields and learning new skills like speaking, writing, marketing, and management. This led to an average of $2,484 per month in improved cash flow per participant. Four out of five people saved on taxes; the average savings was $11,833. Some people created digital programs to teach other businesses in their field what they were doing. Others hired employees. There was a myriad of options, but I followed the acceleration-of-cash-flow formula.

Most of these clients believed that they had to live within their means. I agreed but offered a new perspective: "Let's look to be efficient within your means and, most importantly, expand your means."

This didn't work with all participants, only 97% of them. One of the three people lost money with a connection I gave him on a real estate deal. After a few sessions, the other two weren't a good fit for me and I refunded their money. It requires taking responsibility and action—and being coachable—for any of this to work.

Many 401(k) Hoax participants had lost money following the long haul accumulation process. Philip Rojas was one of those people. In his testimonial for the program, he said, "With the recent decline in the stock market, I have experienced significant losses, some realized and some unrealized. Stock market financial advisors promote themselves by stating that they have spread out their risk and that their losses are not as bad as the benchmark. But in this market, there has been nowhere to hide. All sectors have experienced major declines and, unfortunately, I found out the hard way that I have too much money in the stock market."

People who have followed the advice that I'm outlining here have some common characteristics. They narrow their focus, invest in what they know, pay themselves first, keep more of what they make without cutting back, and protect the downside. They build a foundation and mitigate risk. They utilize teams. They learn to do due diligence. They don't rely on themselves alone because they know that they might get emotional about their decisions. (The higher the level of emotion, the lower the financial IQ.) They have people who help them see what could go wrong and the risks involved, something the long haul rarely addresses. When the market is down, the long haul becomes the excuse that removes all responsibility. "Don't worry, you're in it for the long haul." What an excuse. When does the long haul end?

In addition, those who participated in The 401(k) Hoax made a lot of their wealth through their businesses and then stored it in investments.

They didn't invest at the expense of a career and then have those investments pay off eventually.

The investment advice that's out there isn't always worthwhile, and it is often rooted in the long haul myth. Tony Robbins, a brilliant thinker and motivator, took a detour from his expertise to write *MONEY: Master the Game,* which is really a long sales letter. I can save you the time of reading its 700 pages, because it's how to master the middle-class roadmap of the long haul—reduce expenses through cheaper retirement plans and index funds, start early, and then meet this group of financial people paying Robbins for leads.[6]

I definitely agree on lowering non-performing fees and measuring results, but if you are playing the accumulation game, improvement will be limited. The long haul model isn't even how Robbins made his money. He says that most businesses fail. Guess what? A vast majority of retirement plans fail to provide the desired result of financial independence by age sixty-five. Even if four out of five businesses fail, the odds are still better than doing the retirement planning promoted in that book.

Robbins interviews any number of billionaires in that book. He asks the founder of Vanguard how people get wealthy. The answer: invest in an index fund. Guess what? He is rich because other people invest in his index fund, but he didn't get wealthy investing his money in one. Robbins asks Charles Schwab, and Schwab recommends setting up a discount brokerage account. Schwab profits from selling discount brokerage accounts, but he didn't become a billionaire investing his own money in them.

The same is true of celebrity investment advisors. Suze Orman was exposed at one time for having little investment (around 5%) in the stock market, even though that's a huge part of what she tells others to do. Dave Ramsey didn't make his money by budgeting and investing in the stock market, but by being an amazing businessman. These advisors have their money in things that they know and understand, oftentimes the businesses that they own and control.

If you do read Tony Robbins' book, focus on Ray Dalio, one of the best investors in the world. He talks about teaching himself to minimize and understand risk while producing fantastic returns. Another billionaire in Robbins' book gives fantastic advice: Dr. Marc Farber, creator and publisher of *The Gloom, Boom, & Doom Report,* tells a story consistent with how he made his own money. He says build a business. Find your skill set and expose it to the marketplace in the biggest ways.[7]

Rather than funding everyone else's business or dream, invest in you. Most long haul advice fuels someone else's business, someone else's dream. But what about your life? Your dream? Your Investor DNA?

You don't have to start a business to benefit from this advice. Be intrapreneurial. Find ways you can add to a company's bottom line and get upside potential. Trading time for money and having a salary with no upside, while socking your money away in a retirement plan, leaves potential untapped and limits your ability to be rewarded for the value you create.

Deliberate investment versus automatic investment—"invest early, often, and always" or "set it and forget it"—is key. The wealthiest people automatically save money, wait patiently, and then invest deliberately and at the right time. In 2019, the wealthiest people in the world had an average of 39% of their portfolio moved to cash because they were waiting to pounce on the opportunities.[8] Malcolm Gladwell wrote an article in *The New Yorker* about Ted Turner. A feature of Turner's investment strategy was waiting for distressed times and situations to make a move. He bought land and businesses when people were cash-strapped. He had the patience to wait for those times and keep his liquidity so that when opportunities arose, he could capitalize on them.[9]

## RETHINK THE OTHER LONG HAUL: EDUCATION

Many people equate investing in yourself with formal education. We have wrapped our identities up in a hierarchical system that leads us to believe that the more advanced our degree, the smarter we are. Time in school somehow equals value in society. Many people who don't have a college degree or dropped out of high school let that define them.

We live in a world that has taught us to value perceived education over practical education. We turn our lives over to those with degrees because they are the experts. But what if they are experts in broken systems or limited methodologies, or are learned in something outdated or ineffective—or worse, just peddling a corporate agenda? Look no further than doctors promoting the health benefits of smoking in the 1950s, or later, when I went to school, having nurses and nutritionists with every degree and designation teach us the merits of the food pyramid—really?

To some extent, we've seen through the illusion of equating credentials with value. We've seen pharmaceutical companies turn doctors into customer service representatives. If doctors don't prescribe enough, they'll get lower bonuses, or some pharmaceutical rep will come to scold them and tell them they're not going on that fancy trip.

We want to disrupt these antiquated systems. They don't lead to prosperity or a better life because we are still looking to them for answers rather than finding answers within ourselves. That includes taking time to do what we enjoy for its own sake, not to earn money or get another degree.

Are some of those degrees valuable? Absolutely. Are they as valuable as we've been told? Absolutely not. Finding your value in a piece of paper is very different than having a moment of connected humanity. Were you present with someone, did you see them, did you hear them, were you there for them? We all have that capability if we stop hustling and start seeing what's right in front of us.

If you think that you could never be an expert in all things money, well, that is probably true. I have dedicated almost a quarter century of my life to finance and don't know everything about the tax code, estate planning, tax liens, derivatives, etc. But instead of relying on experts, utilize them. Start by realizing that you have Investor DNA. Know what your values and your competencies are and be clear about what interests you or drives you most. Most retirement planners are better at sales than knowing what will happen with the market. Most people working for a financial institution are selling you on what is best for the institution, not necessarily for you.

You don't have to be an expert in everything or hand over your money to so-called experts without knowing the value or consequence to you. What are you best at? What do you want to learn? What would make the biggest impact on your ability to make more money by adding more value? Start by maximizing your earnings, then focus on efficiency to keep more of what you make. Plug financial leaks by saving on taxes, loan interest, and non-performing investment fees, and design your insurance properly to pay less for your coverage. Then find a way to create cash flow. Don't wait for thirty years to see if this works. There is a better way.

## INVEST IN YOURSELF

I'm a huge advocate for investing in yourself instead of handing your money over to some supposed expert. Are they an expert or just a middleman? Do they know what's going on in the boardroom of any of these investment companies? Or are they simply referencing what's happened over the last thirty years and telling you it's likely to do the same?

Some say, "Just do a Vanguard fund. It has the lowest fees and will give you the best return." Well, guess what? You might not believe in most of the companies in their index.

You might not want those companies to succeed, yet you inadvertently vote for them every single day if you invest your dollars with them.

As I mentioned, I've opted out of the system of funding companies through the stock market. Let me break it down further. First, companies have a fiduciary responsibility to their shareholders. This means that if you're the CEO of a publicly traded company, you have to act in the shareholders' best interest but have no fiduciary responsibility to your employees or your customers. In addition, there is pressure for growth. I'd rather invest in *my* stock, in myself—writing this book, building my business, learning about ways to add value and reach more people. My investments are in intellectual property, not public companies. This is my path, but what is yours? What investments make sense to you? How can you increase your cash flow by the greatest amount? Would it make more sense to pay off loans or hire a mentor first?

## MORE ACCUMULATION IS NOT ALWAYS BEST FOR YOU

One of the best investments for me has always been in my businesses and scaling that revenue. When we use the word *scale,* most people think of scaling up. But you might want to scale down, because scaling up may mean losing what your business stood for in the first place. You may become too corporate, or grow outside of your skill set, or hijack your own life and time. In 2010, my financial firm grew too fast, and I had less of a relationship with our clients. There was more money, but less connection and higher stress.

One construction company that Wealth Factory worked with hired us after going from $40 million to $100 million in just over three years. That sounded amazing, but the owner's life didn't improve with the increase (and that is why he sought out Wealth Factory). Why? It was easy to see after few questions. "Do you spend more or less time with your family now?"

"Much less."

"Are you taking home more money than you did three years ago, or less?"

"Less, because we have more customer complaints and more deadlines and project issues. It's just more than we can manage."

"Great. You get to tell people you're at $100 million in revenue, which is impressive to the world. But you don't have peace of mind; you didn't establish the rules, because the growth came with contractors who are unable to fulfill the promises made by the owner. You have to replace them or step in, which involves time that you would have spent with your family. How often are you on the phone when you're around your family?"

"All the time."

"Great. You thought the win was $100 million, but that had nothing to do with what you really wanted in life. You thought that kind of revenue would mean a better life, but it was actually the opposite."

Sometimes, scaling down can serve you best. It may require reevaluation and pause, which may be less profitable—but only momentarily. Who gets paid when you take time away? It's not great for financial advisors or consultants, but being in nature and finding a hobby are priceless for you, an investment in yourself. There is no commission when people take time to themselves in the short-term.

## VALUE INVESTING

Then there's value investing. Warren Buffett is often admired for investing in companies and stocks that are looking to create value for the long term. Sometimes you'll hear stories about his company, Berkshire Hathaway, buying a business and leaving everything as it is: if it's not broken, why fix it?

But there's a dark side. I have a family member who was a vice president for PacifiCorp, which was bought by Berkshire. After working there for over forty years, he stopped enjoying his work and retired due to Berkshire's "Let's get rid of people and ask other people to pick up the slack" philosophy. Stock price goes up because the company has lowered expenses, but they've asked human beings to do twice the work for the same pay and fewer benefits. These people will have a pension ten years in the future, so they say, "I don't want to lose my pension. I'll do whatever," even at the expense of their humanity. I believe in a free market, but I also see the wealth gap and the middle class having more difficulty making ends meet amidst inflation on purchases, but not on compensation.

This is why I've opted out of the long haul. I haven't had money in the stock market since 2001, and I'm happy with my returns. Some people want it to be easy; they want to hand over their money and not think any more about it, but where else in life does that work? With our health? No. We can't delegate our life to someone else.

The system that Wall Street and the banks use when you give them money is not the long haul and accumulation system. They want to make money on your money. They want to create cash flow. And who takes the risk? YOU!

Let's think about it. Banks have the biggest buildings in every city. What product do they offer? Money. Your money. Not theirs, yours. If they lose the money, what happens? The FDIC comes in and bails them out with the taxes we pay. We're paying ourselves back with our own money.

If you put your money in a savings account, they pay you 1%. Then you turn around and find that you can get a mortgage at 4% interest. If you buy something for a dollar and sell it for four dollars, that's a 400% markup. They're renting your money for a dollar and selling it for four dollars. They're getting a 400% return.

I've seen interest rates at .25%, with mortgage rates at 3%. That's like buying a house and only having to make a $250-a-month payment on it but renting it out for $3,000 a month. Think about that. Can you imagine that kind of cash flow in real estate? You pay $250 and you get $3,000 a month, so that's a profit of $2,750 a month. This is the extraordinary return banks get for being intermediaries.

We're all playing by the banks' rules. We're earning less than they are. Then they want us to believe that if we accumulate for the long haul, we will have a great retirement—while they aim for cash flow.

We think the financial game will work for us, but it's rigged against us. It is working for the banks and Wall Street. They invented the rules. They established their win, and we aren't part of that win. At least they were masked when you went into the bank in 2020–2022, so you knew they were robbing you.

That's the problem with believing it takes money to make money. As you've already learned, money is a by-product of value. It's a by-product of being resourceful, of doing things in the world and being paid for that. Can you find more valuable activities that solve bigger problems, serve more people, or have a deeper impact? That is the game to play.

It may mean that you make less money because your purpose does not call for you to be a billionaire or a millionaire. Could you be happy with that? You could as long as you were not in a state of comparison.

Comparison is the thief of joy. Competition is the breeding ground for scarcity. Scarcity is the game of either-or: someone else gets something, so that means there's less for me.

That's when we cry foul. We want the government to get involved. But the government can't save you; nor is effort enough. Prosperity takes purpose; it takes intention. It takes creating your win and playing your game, even when you're tempted to go off track for something with the promise of a high return.

I've met some people who became worth tens of millions—even hundreds of millions—in cryptocurrency, though they didn't really have a business model. It was more like winning the lottery than a matter of actual skill. But when we let jealousy come in, thinking that should have been us or that somehow the universe did us wrong, we're led astray. We chase returns. When we don't compare ourselves to others, our joy comes from living our purpose.

## THE LONG HAUL IN REAL ESTATE

The worst real estate purchases are rooted in the hope of appreciation over the long haul. You think, *The market's going to up. I'm going to hold on to the property and sell it for more later.* That could change very quickly, though. If interest rates went up right now, the price of real estate could easily decrease because people are buying based more on payment than purchase price. Real estate bubbles come from cheap and easy funding. Low payments or interest rates create a bubble. These times are unique due to limited supply combined with low interest rates, but things can change with a changing economy and especially if borrowing becomes more difficult.

Bubbles themselves can create opportunities for investors. Sometimes it's too expensive for most of the population to buy a new a home. We saw that happen in Southern California, where less than 9% of people could afford a mortgage in 2007. In such situations, rent prices go up for certain homes, so you can profit from apartment development.

On the other hand, in 2008 in Miami, people were stuck with condos they couldn't sell, because only investors and people who wanted second homes were buying them; most buyers weren't actually going to live there, and there weren't enough potential residents.

You have to understand basic supply and demand and the actual value proposition of what you're looking into. Why is this going up in value? Why is this valuable? Whom is this valuable for, and how long will it be that valuable for them?

> **Value Proposition**
>
> **The clearly-defined identification of how value is created for others through specific actions, investments, business proposals, etc. A good value proposition comes in the form of a very clear and concise guiding statement that explains how value is being created and how it will be sustained.**

In real estate, my philosophy leans toward making money on the buy. Make sure it's cash-positive from day one. Or maybe there are a few aspects of the property to improve immediately that increase the value beyond what was paid, or you can buy it from someone in a distressed situation. I've worked with real estate investors whose entire strategy is to send out letters to find people who are struggling or overextended. They help them liquidate properties quickly because they have cash. The owners may end up selling for less than they would if they put money into renovations, but they don't have the time, the money, or (likely) the expertise for that, plus they're too stressed anyway.

Investors can make a lot of money this way, but they also give value to the sellers, who would have had to give the properties back to the bank.

If there is negative cash flow on your property, have you thought about other ways to create cash flow? How about an Airbnb strategy? It'll be more time and effort, but you may be able to use Airbnb to create a positive cash flow. Or have you thought about selling your property with seller financing?

If you're going to get involved in real estate, pick a lane. Don't decide, *I'm going to do some commercial, some single family, and some fix-and-flips.* Get very good at one thing in a concentrated area. Once you have some profits, you can educate yourself in other areas.

All real estate is not equal. There are many strategies, and it would be hard to be great at all of them. First, join an organization where you can learn from others and invest in your education. Then ask, is this what you want to spend your time on? Are you built to be a landlord?

When I was a landlord, I had some tenants who stole copper wire and others who never paid their rent because they knew the rules that allowed them to stay for free for months. In certain states, it's nearly impossible to evict someone (although other states are friendlier toward the landlord).

You've got to know what you're doing. Some people make a lot of money in real estate, but just as many, if not more, lose a lot of money because they do it passively and part-time. They don't have full knowledge; they've just heard that their friends are doing well in real estate or that it's a good time to get involved in it.

I have no passion for most real estate, although many gurus say that you've got to be in real estate to be wealthy. I have picked the lane of investing in one specific development I know well—the homes near my cabin, with riverfront and limited options to build more property, in a place where it is rare to find a property for sale. This is what I know. This is what I stick to.

Be careful with real estate. I'm sure you have seen the many infomercials that tell you you can fix and flip a property and make a lot of money. You don't even have to worry about being a landlord; you can manage everything through management companies. But are the people who tell you this making their money on real estate or on selling you on buying real estate?

Real estate is overhyped far too often. If you're not willing to pay your dues by taking the time and expense to educate yourself, and if you're not saying no to more deals than you're saying yes to, you are in danger. Many people trying to invest in real estate don't belong in real estate because they treat it as a part-time, passive activity, but they're competing against people who *do* have real estate in their Investor DNA.

If you know very little about real estate, it's a terrible investment for you. It's even worse if you temporarily make money and think you're better than you are. Then you're susceptible to overextension and over-leveraging, and at risk of suffering from market changes like those that happened in 2000 and 2008. It's like thinking you can play in the NBA because you practice shooting hoops in your driveway a couple of times a week. If a couple of NBA players showed up to your house and challenged you to a game, you'd get your butt kicked.

Sometimes you know just enough to experience a "win" and think that makes you an expert. It's like playing poker—in Las Vegas. You know the game pretty well, but you don't know that you're sitting down with the world champion poker player. The champion lets you build up false confidence until you get enough drinks in you and chips on the table. They're going to take those chips from you, and you're going to go back home with a story of how you lost money.

Again, that money wasn't lost; it was transferred through what I call the ignorance tax. Many who don't know their Investor DNA pay the most expensive tuition possible. They learn the lesson in the hardest way because they thought real estate was easier than it is and confused *lucky* with *good*.

## FOCUS ON CASH FLOW

If you aren't sure where to invest, start by paying off inefficient loans and improving your cash flow. Look to build cash reserves by saving money you would otherwise pay to those loans. When you have saved up enough cash, take advantage of opportunities that align with your Soul Purpose. Invest in yourself.

Find ways to transfer risk and protect your downside. One way to do this is with insurance, if you design it to your advantage (more on how to do that in Chapter Eleven). Maybe you have duplicate coverages or costs. Focus on efficiency first and recover those costs. Plug the leaks and put that money in your pocket. Either get educated or hire someone who can help you become more educated. Find money that is rightfully yours before you put it into a retirement plan that's locked until you're nearly sixty, produces no cash flow, and has exorbitant fees, including front-end loads.

Increase your financial intelligence and create recurring revenue/cash flow. Create your foundation by saving, taking time to discover who you are, and putting money into yourself, your education, and your most important skill sets. If you pay off loans, save money with overfunded cash value insurance (more on this in Chapter Eleven), and never invest in anything else, you'll be ahead of 95% of the rest of America.

## YOU WERE BORN FOR GREATNESS

One of the best ways to break through the stronghold of popular myths is to make our purpose bigger than we think *we* are. We must start dreaming and thinking big again, the way we used to do as children. We must spend time in the realm of possibility, then strive harder to bridge the gap between our vision and reality. Deep down, all of us know that we were born to do so much more than accumulate a million dollars and retire after thirty years of an uninspired and uninspiring career.

In the words of author Marianne Williamson, "Our deepest fear is not that we are inadequate. Our deepest fear is that we are powerful beyond measure . . . We ask ourselves, 'Who am I to be brilliant, gorgeous, talented, fabulous?' Actually, who are you not to be? Your playing small does not serve the world . . . As we are liberated from our own fear, our presence automatically liberates others."[10]

The myth of the long haul is rooted in handing our potential over to other people—to Wall Street, to gurus, to banks, to so-called experts. Stop letting them define your life, your worth, your future.

Jon Butcher is the chairman of the Precious Moments Family of Companies and the founder of Lifebook. He is also one of my private clients. I'd like to share his words about the shift he made when he started thinking differently about the long haul and other myths, began disrupting his own sacred cows, and stepped into his own greatness.

He said, "Garrett Gunderson taught me a little-known principle that created a complete paradigm shift in my career and my financial life. This principle is contained in the answer to one simple question: **What is my most important asset?** Is it the stock in my companies? My real estate, my securities, my 401(k), the cash I have in the bank? Absolutely not. **My most important asset is ME**. It is my experience, my knowledge, my talents, my character, my relationships, my unique ability to create value for others and prosperity for myself.

"**Understanding that I am my most important asset is a game changer**. It means that the most important thing I could ever invest in is *ME,* and the most important expertise I could ever call on when making an investment or financial decision is **inside myself**. On the surface, this may sound simple and obvious (because it is), but it has the power to completely transform your financial life. I know because it transformed mine. Dig a little deeper, learn it, understand it deeply, and apply it to your life and see what happens."

*You* are your most important asset.

Invest in your most valuable asset: you.

## Chapter Eight

# Myth 5:
# A Penny Saved Is a
# Penny Earned

HAVE YOU STARTED TO NOTICE HOW ONE MONEY MYTH feeds into another? When we believe in the finite pie, that there is only so much money to go around, that feeds into the belief that money is power. If there's only so much of it to go around, then whomever has it has all the power. Those with power (banks, Wall Street, gurus) must know what they are talking about, so we follow, abdicate responsibility, and buy into the myth of the long haul. That myth contributes to a desire to save every penny we can so we can invest more in a mythical future we may never realize.

| MYTH: | REALITY: |
|---|---|
| Myth: Price is what matters more than anything else. Don't spend your money if you can avoid it—except, of course, if you find a good deal! | Price is a small concern relative to value. Focus primarily on value and you will make and save more money in the long run. |

All of the money myths are connected to the core myth: scarcity. That plays out in the common belief that a penny saved is a penny earned. When we focus on saving every penny, price becomes our main concern, not value. The truth is, value is a far more important consideration than price when it comes to purchases and investments. But if we don't value ourselves, develop our skill sets, or take the time to discover our Investor DNA, we limit our ability to create value and build wealth.

## FOCUS ON VALUE

Since its publication, I've heard from many *Killing Sacred Cows* readers. Often, their messages relate to the way they think about saving and spending. One reader, Tom Martin, wrote to me saying, "This book was mind-shattering when it comes to the way we think about our money and our lives. For years, I drove past the coffee shop in the morning thinking that the $1.25 was not well spent, that I'd have to live the way my Depression-era parents did: hoard and not spend."

Once Tom shifted his thinking about scarcity and related myths, he increased his revenue by five times more than he had earned during the same period the year before, in the worst market in seventy years.

The idea that price should be the most important consideration in our financial decisions goes way beyond a morning coffee. It is a destructive myth that limits our potential and keeps us from our Soul Purpose. Furthermore, when we fall prey to this belief, we keep other people away from their Soul Purpose. When we are overly concerned about price, we adopt a do-it-yourself mentality that shuts off the option of utilizing other people's abilities. Focus on price sacrifices quality and value on the altar of stagnation and mediocrity; it prevents us from seeing abundant possibilities. It leads to damaging forms of saving and spending. And if taken too far, it dictates our decisions and the quality of our lives. Ultimately, it limits our ability to see ourselves as valuable.

We can overcome this myth by tapping into our human life value and thinking outside of the limitations of price, focusing more on value than on price, recognizing and utilizing the difference between price and cost (economic impact), and using our purchasing decisions to create the world in which we want to live.

Our human life value is the root of our prosperity; we are our own greatest assets. Our material resources and money are the fruits of prosperity, not the roots. The stronger our roots, the wider our branches and the more abundant our fruit.

> **Human Life Value**
>
> *Human life value is your own particular combination of knowledge, skills, and abilities—everything you are when you take away all of your material resources. It is your character and integrity, your unique ability to think creatively, your relationships, your faith—or the lack of these things. It is your knowledge, and your ability to shape materials and information in new ways that are valued and utilized by you and others.*

## BUDGETING: A SACRED COW

To save more pennies, we turn to budgets, but budgeting is not very effective. This is why budgeting is another sacred cow born of the "a penny saved is a penny earned" mentality. I know that some people are excited to read this and others think this statement is reckless, but stay with me. In her article for *Time*, "The 1 Task Americans Just Can't Accomplish," Martha C. White showed some telling statistics on budgeting.[11] Budgeting is like dieting. Many dieters eventually end up gaining weight because they restrict and restrict. They miss out. They're stressed, obsessed, and frustrated. Eventually, they have a bad day and the diet goes out the window. When I was dieting, my weight fluctuated, and I was always frustrated about food. Since I stopped dieting, I'm leaner and life is better.

Dieting is scarcity thinking. Budgeting is scarcity thinking. The solution is to set up a separate bank account called a *wealth capture account*. This could be a checking, savings, or money market account. You currently have a personal account or business account. Every time you make a deposit, you want an automatic sweep into the wealth capture account so you pay yourself first. This isn't new; it goes back to George S. Clason's book *The Richest Man in Babylon* from the 1920s.[12] Pay yourself first.

You may be familiar with Parkinson's law, that work will expand to fill the time allotted for its completion. This law also applies to money. Our expenses will expand to use up the available money. We see this all the time. When someone gets a raise, their expenses increase to meet or exceed that raise within three to six months because there's no plan for how to spend the additional money. That would seem to be a good argument to budget, but budgeting can create scarcity, limiting production and value. If you want to use increases in income to grow wealth, pay yourself first—before you pay your expenses.

Pay yourself first. Build that peace-of-mind fund. Have at least enough liquidity or savings to handle six months' worth of expenses. Preferably, you'll save up to nine or twelve months' worth, or even enough to cover you for two years, but don't stress yourself out with that objective.

When you have more than six months' worth of expenses saved, you can consider investing that money or paying off loans. All you do is automatically save that amount each time you deposit money and then, once a week or every other week, depending on your personality, look and make sure you didn't spend more than came in.

## FOUR KINDS OF EXPENSES

While budgeting is an ineffective tool for growing wealth, it does help to look at your expenses and decide if they are worth it. Most people treat all expenses in the same way. When there's a cash crunch, they start cutting some of the wrong things. Instead of budgeting, pay yourself first and then classify your expenses; some you may increase, and others you may want to cut.

There are four types of expenses. The first is *destructive expenses:* borrowing to consume. A college student sees a cute girl giving away free T-shirts with a credit card that charges 29% interest. He gets the card, spends money on stuff he doesn't need, and now he owes it. Another destructive expense: borrowing to fill the gap. For example, you don't have money to go on a trip, but you go anyway. When you come back, you have the memories of the trip, but you also have a loan that puts pressure on you. Eliminate destructive expenses.

Then there are *lifestyle expenses.* Lifestyle expenses are a normal part of life; just pay cash for them. Don't borrow to consume.

The third type is *protective expenses:* asset protection, estate planning, insurance, building up liquidity, and education.

Understanding protective expenses is the difference between the ultra-wealthy and the middle class. The ultra-wealthy know how to manage risk and mitigate it. Most people in the middle class think they've got to take risk to get return, which is a huge lie. The notion that high risk equals high return makes no sense. How in the world does increasing your chance of losing help you win? (More about this in Chapter Ten.)

To reduce risk, it is imperative to transfer risk and know how your investments work. Part of your protective expense is in education. Learn to be a better investor. When you know your Investor DNA, you only invest in what you know. Let me reiterate: risk is not in the investment; it is in you, the investor. If you invest in something that you know nothing about, you increase and invite risk. If you do not have an exit strategy or know what value the investment creates in the marketplace, you are speculating. Investing in yourself and creating a process to understand and manage risk will make you a better investor.

Banks mitigate risk. If they don't, they lose money. Back in the early 2000s, they offered things like stated income loans: you don't actually have to make the money, just say that you do. We saw a major implosion because banks stopped managing risk. They thought times would always be good and always get better.

The fourth type is *productive expenses,* where you spend one dollar on something and two dollars come out on the other side. You don't budget those expenses. Instead, the plan is to keep putting money in so long as the strategy keeps working and you have the capacity to handle it.

In 2010, I hired a chairman for my company. I gave him half the salary he wanted. I said, "Here's half. Find the other half." He was able to do this because he's brilliant at finding inefficiencies and improving margins, and he accomplished it within six months. It was a totally productive expense because paying him freed up my time. I removed things from my calendar that I could trust him with and that I wasn't even that good at. I started doing more productive things. We had a banner year in 2010.

Good employees are a productive expense. Marketing could be a productive expense. Experiences and customer service and support could be productive expenses.

*Killing Sacred Cows* was a productive expense. I'd never written a book. I hired a writing coach. I invested in building a team of editors and researchers. I took out full-page ads in *The New York Times* and *The Wall Street Journal*. I hired a book promoter. I found a publisher. It was an expensive project, but I made much more than I invested after all was said and done.

On the personal side, a productive expense could be taking care of health or spending time with family to feel connected. Anything can become a productive expense if it supports you to create more cash or cash flow than the expense associated with producing the result.

## SAVE 18%

I recommend working toward saving 18% of your income. There's a reason for 18%. I'll break it down: 3% is for inflation (which is still low because inflation is currently much, much higher, but that is accounted for in the following percentages). You'll want 3% for potential tax hikes. Another 3% is for planned obsolescence. Things break down and have to be replaced. Add 3% for technological change: we customarily buy things now that didn't exist ten or twenty years ago. I think that's going to continue at an accelerated rate.

Another 3% is for propensity to consume, which means that a luxury, once enjoyed, becomes a necessity. When you enjoy nicer things, you get nicer taste. I used to think Sizzler was fine dining. I remember staying in cheap motels growing up, but once I stayed in a luxury boutique hotel, there was no going back.

The last 3% is my favorite. I recommend setting up another account and calling it your *living wealthy account:* if you've saved 15% in your wealth capture account, just add another 3% for living wealthy. This account is for guilt-free spending—treating yourself. Think, *I know I'm doing the right things financially, so let me spend this on what I want.*

Your living wealthy account is a reminder that you are doing the right things with your money. You don't have to feel guilty about buying a nice dinner or a nice bottle of wine or whatever enhances your lifestyle based on what you value. In the "penny saved is a penny earned" mindset, it is challenging to focus on quality of life. It creates a scenario that overemphasizes having certain amounts of money in the bank instead of investing in ways to increase your ability to create income.

A lot of people wonder, *How would I save 18%?* That's a big number, I know. With inflation on the rise, it may be hard to set aside income. If you are barely scraping by, how can you find more cash to build up your savings? Focus on efficiency rather than limiting your lifestyle. (In the next chapter, I'll share the four I's for efficiency.) Start by looking at your destructive expenses and cut those. Then find ways to increase your income and expand your means. Focus on progress over perfection. You can allocate more of your money to savings over time.

## Chapter Nine

# Myth 6:
# High Risk = High Returns

I NVESTING WITHOUT INVESTOR DNA, WITHOUT STEWARD-
ship, is gambling. "High risk equals high returns" is a myth that is
part of that mentality; it is a gambling philosophy, not an investing
philosophy.

The best and safest investments are those that align with our passions,
knowledge, and abilities.

| MYTH: | REALITY: |
|---|---|
| Safe investments yield low returns. High returns come from risky investments. | Using your Investor DNA and aligning with your Soul Purpose creates less risk and more return when it comes to investing. |

## THE LOWER THE RISK, THE HIGHER THE REWARDS

When we believe in and act from the myth that high risks translate into
high returns, we compromise sustainability, limit our potential, and keep
ourselves from living our Soul Purpose. This myth aids us in avoiding
responsibility for our investment decisions; it fills our lives with unnecessary fear and worry that prevent us from thinking productively. It ignores
the fact that the individual investor, not the particular product, is the

factor that determines the outcome of investments. This myth leads us toward gambling and away from actual investing, tricks us into following the crowd and suffering from the herd mentality, and prevents us from seeing lost opportunity costs.

> ### Opportunity Cost
>
> *The cost of what you could have done with your money in any particular situation, instead of what you actually did. For example, if you lost $10,000 in an investment, the cost was $10,000. The opportunity cost is what that money could have grown to had it been invested elsewhere.*

To the extent that we educate ourselves to take control of our investments and mitigate risks, we will prosper. The lower our risks, the higher our rewards and the more sustainable our long-term investments will be.

## STRATEGIES OF THE WEALTHY

The wealthiest people are masterful at managing risk. They own nothing but control everything. One way they do this is through asset protection: you can own nothing but still have access to everything.

One tool of the wealthy is the Domestic Asset Protection Trust (DAPT). A trust is a document that determines ownership and treatment of assets. That's right, you don't own them because the trust does. You designate a distribution trustee who reports to you so you can protect the assets and still have access to the cash.

The DAPT is used to keep creditors from reaching the trust's assets without preventing you from being able to access your money. This is a tool popularized by the Rockefellers. Their asset protection shields them so that it's never really known how much they truly have.

It doesn't stop there. The Rockefellers even have their own financial team. It includes financial professionals who cohesively and comprehensively work together for the family. This is instrumental in reducing risk.

Rather than speculate, these professionals emphasize key areas that can generate immediate benefit with little to no risk.

One example is tax savings. It's one of the biggest opportunities, as taxes are a major expense. We've heard stories about billionaires not paying income tax. This is only part of the story, because income tax is only one kind of tax; there are any number of others. And there are ways to reclassify income and save money depending on, for example, the chosen type of entity, the way payment is received, or the classification of the asset as capital gains versus ordinary income (to name a few).

Entrepreneurs and small businesses have many of the same advantages as the ultra-wealthy. The wealthy do have access to private banks and can design sophisticated insurance strategies that middle-class people don't have access to, though. The wealthiest people can use private placement life insurance or premium finance, whereby a bank will lend them money to fund tax-favored life insurance programs. They might pay 1.25% to the bank in order to fund an insurance plan that could earn a cash value of 3%, 4%, or higher. The middle class can't design things exactly that way, but my book *What Would Billionaires Do?* shows people how to mimic those strategies. As part of your purchase of *Disrupting Sacred Cows,* you can also download a complimentary copy of *What Would Billionaires Do?* at WealthFactory.com/disrupting.

**Four I's for Efficiency**

IRS  ·  *Investments*  ·  *Insurance*  ·  *Interest*

## THE FOUR I's

Instead of taking more risk with your money, first learn to keep more of what you make. This can support financial security by improving your cash flow. Before you scrimp and budget, find money to put into your life. In my experience, 10% or more of people's income is lost to inefficiency: not understanding financial philosophy, tipping the government, and paying too much to financial institutions.

There are four I's that create efficiency. The first *I* is the *IRS*. Many people are tipping the government. I don't think we should be tipping the government. I'd rather pay them what I owe legally and ethically and keep the rest. But because people don't have a proper, proactive strategy around taxes, they end up overpaying.

Some people intentionally overpay to get a refund.

At one of our Wealth Factory workshops, a man named Brian shared that he had overpaid by $110,000 but didn't get his refund, so he tried to get ahold of the IRS. It was during the pandemic, when people called the IRS and the automated system told them to call back due to high demand every time. Even accounting professionals who had a direct line couldn't get through, often after being on hold for more than forty-five minutes.

It took Brian over a year beyond the normal time required for resolution to get the money. He was really concerned. It was fortunate that he finally got ahold of a caring employee who eventually navigated what had happened and got him his check. In the meantime, he was giving an interest-free loan to the government. If you don't pay the IRS on time, there's a 9% charge. If you overpay them, they just give you your money back—eventually.

## Investments and Insurance

The second *I* of economic efficiency is *investments*. It's not just about how much you earn. Sure, you want to do your best, but not at the expense of taking too much risk or losing peace of mind. It's about finding the inefficiencies, the nonperforming fees, and other things that don't add to the bottom line.

Many studies show that over twenty years, index funds beat managed funds most of the time. This is especially true of non-hedge funds, which are what the masses are putting money into (in their IRAs or 401(k)s). Actively managed funds have a myriad of fees that are often dismissed as minimal. These seemingly small fees end up having a compounding cost effect. Instead of thinking in terms of percentages, analyze the impact to your bottom line. The difference between earning

9.2% and 10% over thirty years on $100,000 is $343,162.44. If you earn 10% for thirty years on your $100,000, it grows to $1,744,940.23—versus $1,401,777.79 if you earn 9.2%. Percentages count. Find those expenses that are not adding to performance and remove them to keep more of what you make.

The third *I* of efficiency is *insurance*. There are a lot of duplicate coverages with insurance, and instances of improper structuring. The highest cost for insurance is for the first dollar of coverage; the least is for the last. People are paying to insure things that they can afford to replace on their own. If they start insuring only catastrophic losses, they'll get more bang for their buck by getting more coverage and/or paying less in premiums. They can put that money in their savings accounts, which can handle the small things. In *What Would Billionaires Do?,* my coauthor and I did a comparison and analysis and found that it's up to 400% better to plug the financial leaks and keep money stable while earning half the interest rate than to double the interest rate.

## Managing Interest

The fourth *I* is *interest*. There are three Rs that can help you lower your interest. One is *restructuring*. Many people have an improper loan structure. Here's an example. Someone has a 12% interest rate on their credit card, but they have a car that's paid off. Why not refinance that car at 1.9% and pay off the 12% credit card?

This strategy accomplishes a couple of things. First, it will boost your credit score. A car loan is an amortized loan; if you pay on time, it helps your credit score. But if you've maxed out your credit card or your loan to value or utilization rate, your credit score will go down.

Having a revolving loan, like a credit card, means that you can keep charging it up and paying it down. Going above 30% of your credit limit can lower your credit score. A lower credit score could mean higher interest and insurance rates.

There's also simple restructuring by refinancing because interest rates are so low right now. I don't have any loans other than my mortgage. Although I have the cash to pay it off, we don't plan on staying in that home for a long period of time, and I could earn interest on that capital more effectively and without risk. I have an account that is stable and gets me around 5%. Right now, my mortgage is at 2.75%. I'm earning more, with safety and liquidity.

Another approach is *renegotiating* interest rates. All interest rates are negotiable. If you have a credit card, call the company and ask, "What are your best deals?" or, "I'm thinking about doing a balance transfer, or closing my account." They'll likely transfer you to the retention department, where it's easier to get a lower interest rate.

The third R is *reallocating,* which involves analyzing your savings and investments to look at any underperforming assets. If they're earning less than you're paying in interest elsewhere, cash them out and pay off the loans with higher interest rates; it's a guaranteed savings.

## SHOULD YOU PAY OFF YOUR MORTGAGE?

Before you refinance or pay extra money to the bank in an attempt to pay off your mortgage, let's analyze this important, sensitive topic.

Financial planners are often of two schools of thought regarding mortgages. Some advocate paying off a mortgage as quickly as you can: get rid of it. Others advise carrying a long-term mortgage and refinancing it regularly, because you're getting the tax benefit as well as the low rates and you can make more money elsewhere.

Let me break this down so you can make an informed decision. The first consideration is, how do you feel about having a mortgage? Is it stressful? Does it create constant worry? How often do you think about your mortgage in a negative way? What makes economic sense may be at odds with what creates peace of mind. I want you to consider both the economic and the emotional factors.

Remember, you are your greatest asset—not a stock, bond, or piece of real estate. Say you make an investment that could earn a high rate of return, maybe even 20%, but you lose sleep. You fight with your spouse about it. If it preoccupies your mind, you're going to be less productive; you're going to be less healthy and happy. Is it worth it to get that potential rate of return?

My answer is absolutely not. Especially if you're a business owner, in which case the drop in your productivity will show up in your profits. You have to think of that external rate of return, which I've mentioned in regard to savings accounts. Savings might not be earning much, but making less can be worth more peace of mind.

Let me give another example. Rich Christiansen is a close friend and the brilliant author of many books, including *The Zigzag Principle.* He told me that when he left the corporate world, he had an interest rate of less than 3% on his mortgage. He said, "I'm going to start a business."

His wife said, "I'm glad you're going to do that, but can we pay off the mortgage?"

"But it's so cheap, and we can earn more money elsewhere."

"I would just feel better and be able to sleep more easily at night if you pay it off, and that would help me support you even more," she replied.

Rich reluctantly paid it off. And he has now sold nineteen businesses.

How you handle your finances, especially your loans, is something that can impact your overall peace of mind. If my wife thought paying off a loan would make her feel better, I would think of the overall satisfaction and fulfillment over the economics. Even if I felt that I could earn more in an investment, it wouldn't be worth the stress it could cause in our marriage.

I want you to create a life you love, not just the highest possible net worth. Opinions about paying off a mortgage can change with economics. In the 1990s, people said you'd be crazy to pay off a mortgage when you could earn 20% in the stock market. In the 1990s, everybody made money. But in 2000–02, the market came crashing down, as it did again in 2008–10. For a time in 2020, the market came down and then bounced back. How certain is the return on your money that you use to invest versus pay off a loan? The answer depends on your plan, your mindset, and your options. (More on mortgages in Chapter Twelve.)

## THE COST OF MONEY

Another factor to consider when paying off a loan versus investing is the cost of money, also known as *opportunity cost*. What is the highest sustainable rate of return that you can get in the long-term or the highest rate of interest you are paying to borrow money? If you have a credit card at 22%, that's your cost of money. Anytime you spend a dollar and don't pay off the loan immediately, it's really costing you $1.22.

Cost of money is critical in making financial decisions and managing risk. Suppose I'm willing to lend you money and won't charge you any interest. How much do you want? As much as you can get. How fast will you want to pay me back if I let you choose? You'll string it out as long as possible because you know you can earn more than 0% on that money elsewhere. The same would be true for most if I charged 1%. But say I'm going to charge you 20%. Would you agree to that? If you did, you would want to pay me back as fast as possible.

This is the cost-of-money effect. It's exactly how banks work. If you make a deposit in a bank and they pay you 1%, they will never lend that money for less than 1%.

Banks also look at risk mitigation. If you want to get a mortgage, they'll want an appraisal; if it's a jumbo loan, they might want two appraisals (and you pay for appraisals). They look at your taxes. They look at your credit score. If you don't make a big enough down payment, they want PMI (private mortgage insurance). Without enough of a down payment, there is more risk to the bank, so they charge for insurance as a protection.

**Risk Mitigation**

> *Any and all measures designed to reduce the risk of any investment opportunity. Risk mitigation factors include education, analyzing the value proposition, insurance and legal products and strategies, collateralization, aligning with principle, and more.*

In any case, banks will always charge you more interest than they pay to rent the money from someone else. They're in the business of cash flow. They're not taking that money and socking it away in a retirement plan, waiting for thirty years, and hoping that it all works out. They're looking to cash-flow that money immediately.

As of this writing, I've seen people secure mortgage rates as low as 2%. That is an amazing rate—unless you are keeping your cash in money markets and savings accounts. Earning more than 2% might be harder for some people than it is for others. Paying off a loan is a guaranteed savings, whereas the outcomes on investments are not guaranteed. Therefore, a word of caution to those who would allocate the equity of their home to the stock market after cash-out refinancing: the stock market is up and down and likely overvalued, plus there are fees and potential taxes that cut into the net return.

Volatility impacts overall return as well. Say I put $100,000 into a fund. Over the first year, it loses 10%. I'm now at $90,000 (assuming there are no fees). The next year, it gains 10%. But it didn't for me, because I was at $90,000, and 10% of 90,000 is $99,000—not even the $100,000 I started with. Now I'm two years behind.

Financial advisors love to argue with my YouTube videos by stating that over the long-term, the stock market has averaged an annual rate of return of 10%. But the reality is, from 2000 to 2015, the actual rate of return of the stock market adjusted for inflation was 8.7% (total), counting the down years of 2000 to 2002 and 2008 to 2010.

To make matters worse, in an article I wrote for *Forbes,* I cited a study showing that during the last twenty years, 10% of investors realized 84% of the gains.[13] That's because we're dealing with hedge funds, which have different rules than the average fund. As noted in his article for BetterInvesting, "Market Madness," Dennis Genord explains,

> Short selling a stock is a trading strategy that speculates on the decline in a stock's price. It's a strategy that should only be utilized by experienced (and some might say pessimistic) traders. Typically with short selling, a trader opens a position by borrowing shares of a company from a broker-dealer. To open a short position, a trader must have a margin account that allows investors to borrow

money to buy securities. Traders will typically have to pay interest on the value of the borrowed shares while their position is open. To close a short position, a trader buys the shares back on the market and returns them to the broker-dealer.

Their hope is that the price paid for the shares to close the position is less than the price they borrowed the shares at. The difference between the amount borrowed and the amount paid to close the position reflects the profit or loss experienced by the trader. Interest charged, commissions and other charges must be taken into account by the trader as these will eat into the potential profits or increase the losses depending on the situation.[14]

It's complicated for anyone who hasn't dedicated their career to the financial industry. People usually just hand over their money while relying on partial information and sound bites. So a hedge fund may get a 9% return while the average investor gets 3%, yet it is reported that the market went up 6%. This is a rudimentary explanation to prove a point, but is it worth the risk and volatility to get a subpar return?

As for mutual funds, say it's 2008 and you get into a growth objective mutual fund. Your fund managers don't want to purchase most growth stocks because they're overvalued and the market is going down, but they can't move that money to cash. They have to stay in growth funds because growth is the objective.

Jeffrey Vinik worked for Fidelity, managing money for its Magellan fund. In the late 1990s, he moved money in stocks to bonds and cash because he felt the market was overvalued. He was right, but Fidelity was sued because that fund has a strict objective. Vinik then started a hedge fund instead.

## FEES

Many people who have mortgages are in the game of refinancing as rates drop. But there are many fees associated with refinancing. When you start signing on a mortgage, you want to look at your origination fee, which could range from .25% to as high as 2%—and that's of the total mortgage. Sometimes it's wrapped into the mortgage, so people don't think about it, but it does raise their principal.

Then you've got the title fees, the title search, and, most importantly, back-end points. Back-end points mean that if the mortgage broker sells you a higher interest rate, they get more points on the back end. You don't see this when you write a check up front, but you pay a higher interest rate than you would if they didn't have those back-end points.

You can see all the costs of a refinance. Recently, when I did a refinance and got my interest rate down to 3% from 4%, it cost me $13,000. It saves me a little over $1,200 a month. If I wasn't going to stay in that house for a year, it wouldn't make sense. Then there's all the time it takes to do a refinance, gathering documents and going back and forth with underwriters. Your time has value.

Could I earn more than 1.9% (or 0%) if I financed a car at that rate and invested the money instead of just writing a check for the car? Maybe, but the bottom line is, I like not having the payment. I like writing a check and leaving the lot, so I'm not dealing with financing.

## DUE DILIGENCE

You can safely improve cash flow by plugging your leaks, but "high risk equals high return" is primarily a myth around how to manage money. Improving returns without increasing risk is about becoming a better investor. Stick to investments that are congruent with your Investor DNA. Build a process and structure for analyzing and mitigating risk.

To help you manage risk, I'll share my list of the ten questions I wish I would have asked before I invested in my early real estate portfolio. These questions ask you to consider your Investor DNA, which enables you to reduce risk and save time by avoiding pitches and investments that aren't aligned with who you are. (You can get this free due diligence tool, the Investor Scorecard, at WealthFactory.com/scorecard.) The Investor Scorecard isn't a risk assessment because most risk assessments aren't that helpful. I know this a bold statement, but think about it: what if I ask you, on a scale of zero to five, how much risk you are willing to take? If you believe that risk equals return, you're likely to say five. But if I asked you the day after you lost everything, you'd punch me. Zero. How is asking these types of questions useful in assessing risk?

After you use the Investor Scorecard, get an outside perspective from someone who is not attached to the outcome. I've got my attorney; I've got my chairman, Norm, who bought my company; and I've got a few other advisors in specific situations who help me do due diligence. Otherwise, my emotions can create risk; I tend to get excited and don't always have patience, and details are not my strength. My advisors poke holes in my arguments and help me understand the risks, so if I decide to go ahead with a deal, we mitigate those risks before we make the move. This changes the game of finance.

This vetting approach especially applies to cryptocurrency, which normally increases the size of the greed gland. There are plenty of faux experts in cryptocurrency. One popular cryptocurrency, Dogecoin, does not even have a development team. There's nothing going on there. It's pure speculation—a pump-and-dump strategy. There are no fundamentals.

Increasing your risk creates a higher chance of loss. If you are investing in things you don't understand, chasing returns without knowing your exit strategy, speculating on long-term growth without considering cash flow, or allocating money based upon fear or greed, you are taking on risk. Instead, create your due diligence process, discover your Investor DNA, invest in yourself, and seek to be a lifelong learner in order to become a better investor.

## Chapter Ten

# Myth 7:
# Self-Insurance

WHAT "SELF-INSURANCE" REALLY MEANS IS NO INSURANCE. The best way to reduce your insurance expenses is to design your insurance properly. You do this by focusing on catastrophic coverage and transferring the risks that matter.

**Self-Insurance**

*The belief that if a person has enough assets accumulated in the bank or in another safe, liquid account, they can drop all of their insurance to save money on premiums and make up for unforeseen losses with their own assets. There is no such thing as self-insurance; either you have insurance or you don't.*

MYTH:
*Spend as little on insurance as possible; it's nothing but a drain on your resources.*

REALITY:
*Get the best insurance you can. When understood, it decreases your risk and increases your productivity.*

## THE CHEAPEST INSURANCE

Improperly designed insurance can be expensive, especially if you haven't properly transferred risk and remain exposed. In *Killing Sacred Cows*, the self-insurance chapter created an understanding of how to use insurance to protect your assets and free up your money to invest rather than tie it up for self-insurance (a.k.a. indemnify losses with your own funds). Meaning that not being insured—or self-insuring anything catastrophic—limits the use of your funds, as you likely have to keep a certain amount of money safe and liquid. If you don't have the personal funds in position to handle a claim, you take on risk and an incident can create strain on your life and finances.

The main reasons people are uninsured, or underinsured, is that they either want to save money on insurance premiums or simply don't know what they actually have. It is easy to see why people have outdated coverage or unnecessary exposure. I don't think most people wake up in the morning and think, *Hey, I should look at my insurance policies and talk to my agent, that sounds like fun!* Insurance is usually something we think about after something happens to us or someone we know. If we hear of major damage to someone's car or home, it may cause us to wonder if we have the right coverage—especially if part of the story is about how the insurance company didn't cover what was expected.

Some insurances are required by law, but most are optional. You can choose to carry or drop your homeowner's insurance if you don't have a mortgage. But if you choose to save the money by not getting insurance, you are responsible for any losses with the home. A catastrophic incident like a house fire would require a substantial amount of capital to repair or replace the home. Maybe you save $2,000 a year in premiums on a $500,000 home, but if you don't have insurance, you might choose to keep $500,000 somewhere safe and liquid (without the opportunity for growth or high interest). Say you have the insurance: how much could you earn on the $500,000 since you are free to invest it where you choose? If you could get even 3% on your

$500,000, you could pay the $2,000 premium and still have $13,000 left over with the return on your money.

The cheapest insurance comes from properly designed policies that insure the catastrophic items, not the inconsequential ones. Something is inconsequential if you have the money to pay for it today and can rest easy without feeling like you have harmed your overall financial plan. Cheapest insurance doesn't mean the lowest premium, but insurance that serves you with the ability to transfer risk efficiently. Companies that specialize in risk management and can pool risk are much cheaper than "self-insurance." Using your own funds means you pay at least a dollar for each dollar of self-insurance. You have to lock up that dollar and miss out on the potential interest it could earn in investments that may not be as liquid. When you buy insurance from a company, you are definitely paying less than a dollar for each dollar of coverage. When designed properly, it should be pennies on the dollar.

Get the best insurance, free up your capital, and create peace of mind, and that will be your cheapest way to insure. Use protection to enhance your production. Knowing you have properly protected yourself and your assets and managed your risk creates a real sense of security.

## INSURANCE STRATEGY

In the spirit of determining the cheapest/best way to insure, let's investigate life insurance. The common belief among retirement planners is that you should buy term insurance instead of whole life. Term insurance is promoted as cheaper, meaning that it has a lower premium up front, and you can invest the difference. It also has no cash value and covers you for a specified term. While you make your premium payments, you have insurance. When your payments stop, your coverage does too. There are level term policies that keep your premiums steady for ten, twenty, or thirty years, or annual renewable term insurance plans that can increase the premium year by year. Over life expectancy, term insurance premiums can be greater than the death benefit because their price increases over time. Simply put, the more likely you are to die based upon actuarial tables as you age, the higher the premium.

> ### Term Life Insurance
>
> *Life insurance that provides a death benefit for a certain period of time. Unlike permanent life insurance, term life insurance carries no cash value within the policy and has no tangible living benefits.*

Term insurance has only two benefits. The first is peace of mind from knowing that if something happens to you, your family will be financially okay. The second is, the cash comes in income tax-free if you die. Every other benefit is removed with term insurance. It is useful as a placeholder, a stopgap measure, but it is based on price and price alone and limited in the long-term.

With the "buy term and invest the difference" philosophy, people are encouraged to have insurance until they have enough assets to replace the coverage, just as in the homeowner's policy example. This leads people to live off of their interest rather than utilize their assets or spend their principal. As mentioned in earlier chapters, this leaves them susceptible to interest rate decreases, tax fluctuations, and inflation, all of which confiscate their purchasing power.

> ### Permanent Life Insurance
>
> *Permanent life insurance policies are designed to provide coverage for the duration of a person's lifetime, not just a specified term. They carry a cash value that accrues with premiums paid, and provide many benefits that a policyholder has access to while living, such as tax protection and disability protection, among others.*

Whole life insurance is a permanent insurance plan that includes cash value and has a fixed premium payment, guaranteed death benefit, and guaranteed interest rate. It is often viewed as more expensive because the up-front premium is much higher than term insurance. At eighteen, I was told that whole life was a hole you throw your money into. And given the majority of insurance companies and their policy design, I can see why people believed this. Commission-heavy and cash-light limits cash and performance. The longer it takes for cash to show up or the policy to break even, the worse the policy can be for you. There is a different way to design, use, and benefit from a whole life policy.

The best way to think about insurance is outside the binary of term versus whole. Rather than think of it as a choice between the two, think of it as a strategy that utilizes different approaches at different points in your life.

Too often, people buy whole life without considering the death benefit amount or how to protect their economic value (earnings over their lifetime), thereby leaving their family exposed if something happens to them. Life insurance is about indemnification: if I were to die, it would replace the income my family would have had if I had lived—at least to some degree. Be careful not to chase cash value over coverage. Whole life can have more benefits in most instances, but focus on protection first.

**Indemnification**

*Compensation for damage or loss sustained, expense incurred, etc. Also, guarding or securing against anticipated loss, or providing security against future damage or liability. Self-insurance provides no means of indemnification; proper insurance covers losses without the individual policyholder needing to replace items out of pocket that were lost through unforeseen events.*

If you don't know what kind of life insurance to own, term is the right one for you, for now. Simply put, if you aren't sure what you're doing, or are struggling with cash flow, you can get coverage today with term insurance.

Mutual fund salespeople have told the masses to buy term and invest the difference because they are focused on getting paid for assets under management like mutual funds. Other people, who are making more money on life insurance, tell us to buy life insurance. You have two divergent philosophies, but both sellers of mutual funds and sellers of life insurance have to ask the client what the client is trying to accomplish. How does it all fit together? Are there ways to transfer and reduce risk while still enhancing a return?

If you buy term for now, make sure that term is convertible to a whole life policy when you have a better understanding or improved cash flow. When I talked with an actuary at a massive life insurance company in New York City, he told me that only 1.1% of term policies ever pay out. Since we are all guaranteed to die, I want a policy that is around one more day than I am; so, over time, I converted all my term insurance to whole life.

*Killing Sacred Cows* gives the philosophical argument for this strategy in the chapter called "Self-Insurance." In my book *What Would Billionaires Do?*, I discuss the practical implementation of properly designed whole life. We're disrupting the entire nature of insurance so that it's something that benefits you while you're alive rather than only when you die.

I started buying insurance when I was nineteen years old. I bought term and also put fifty dollars a month into a whole life policy. As my income increased, I converted my term into whole life. Here we are, twenty-four years later, and my whole life has never failed me. When the market went down, it didn't. When my policy wasn't performing as well as other opportunities that presented, I utilized the cash value in my whole life policy to put down payments on real estate. I used it to build a TV studio when my team created our first digital products and educational courses. I used it to pay off an American Express account with a higher interest rate. I used it to buy a cabin. I didn't have to lock up the money until I was fifty-nine-and-a-half, as I would have had to do with an IRA or 401(k). I didn't have to worry when there were market downturns or pandemics. I didn't lose any sleep or have any of the stress that comes with market volatility. I haven't had to pay any tax on any of the gains, either. I have a multitude of benefits, like liability protection and disability protection (if I become disabled and can't make the payments, the insurance company continues the deposits for me). Through a feature called the accelerated benefit rider, I can tap into my death benefit while I'm alive if I ever need long-term care.

The internal return on my whole life policies has been around 4% on cash value. Some of my oldest policies have done slightly better and some of my newer policies have been lower. But there are other benefits that add to my overall external return. For example, I don't have to pay for term insurance. I pay no tax on the cash value, and I can access it along the way without penalty. I can even coordinate other non-cash flow assets with my death benefit to create more cash flow. (For more on this concept, download *What Would Billionaires Do?* at WealthFactory.com/disrupting.) The Rockefellers, one of the wealthiest families in the world and one that has maintained family wealth for generations, buy life insurance on all of their heirs. When they die, the life insurance replenishes the trust, so this is a key strategy in perpetuating wealth and creating a family bank.

## WHOLE LIFE AND PENSION FUNDS

To coordinate your death benefit with other assets to create more cash flow, let's explore how companies have done this over the years (and you can too).

General Electric (GE) used this strategy well. In the 1950s, GE wanted to hire top talent. To recruit this talent, they said, "We'll give you a pension if you work with us for a certain number of years." That was something these employees weren't being offered by the companies they were with, so GE recruited the best. As soon as someone came to work for them, GE bought a whole life policy on them, which built cash value.

They could use that cash value to either pay for the employee's pension or supplement it because it was stable, predictable, and secure. The cash value was used to fund part or all of the pension, and when the employee died, the death benefit came back to GE tax-free. So not only did GE have the ability to recruit talent and pay for or supplement the pension, they could also create a recovery of the pension cost with a positive, tax-free rate of return upon the employee's death.

In later years, when the stock market was doing so well, Wall Street executives lured GE by saying, "Put your money in the market. You're going to get a better rate of return, and at least double the return you would get on your cash value." Great—except the returns were removed due to market downturns and pensions were compromised.

We saw pensions bankrupt companies and employees who were no longer able to receive what was promised. Risk does not equal return. Not all plans are created equal, and certainty has an economic value.

The stock market was all over the place in the early 2000s, and pensions were compromised. Many of them went bankrupt. All of a sudden, companies had to pay the pensions they'd committed to, but the funds weren't growing anymore because they had started to do what's called *disinvesting*. Investing is when we put money in and it grows. Disinvesting happens in the distribution phase. When the market goes down but there is still a distribution, losses accelerate and destroy the fund.

When disinvesting utilizes funds from a volatile account, the funds may be extinguished. How much can you safely take from a volatile account invested in the stock market? One year you make 12%, and next year you could be at 0%. The following year, you might make 15%. The next year, you might lose 10%. Even though the gain might average 8% over the long-term, *average* and *actual* are two different things.

During the 0% and −10% years, there is a compounded negative effect: first, from not earning and the opportunity cost of a year without growth, and second, from dipping into the funds to cover obligations to the beneficiaries.

With volatility, funds are invaded for distribution during down years, and with less money in the funds, they have less money earning interest.

Therefore, the funds might be unable to meet long-term obligations for the pensions, putting companies at risk. During the 2008 recession, rules in some states still required that pensions be paid before employees. That was the demise of some companies.

## A FINANCIAL LEGACY

Look at whole life as a part of sustaining a financial legacy. Having the death benefit come in and replenish what you've spent in retirement allows for money to be kept in trust so the next generation isn't born into financial bondage.

This is the strategy of the Rockefeller family, and it has enabled them to preserve and increase their wealth over several generations. One caveat is that heirs are not guaranteed any inheritance. Instead of an inheritance, there is a family bank. I use whole life for my family bank because it has cash value and a death benefit. Rather than store my money in savings, where it is taxable, low-interest, and without a death benefit, I prefer to overfund whole life. I can use the cash value anytime I want. After I die, my family bank is funded with a tax-free death benefit in my trust. I set up policies on all my heirs. If they want to borrow from this cash value (owned by the trust), they can. The cash can be used to start a business, make a down payment on a home, finance a car, or acquire other assets; plus, it can happen at a preferred rate. When I cut out the banks and create my own, my family can earn the interest that would normally be paid to these institutions.

I have a board of directors who are identified in my estate plan. They are not compensated while I am alive. My wife and I can make financial choices on our own, but we can also utilize the board, combined with an underwriting process—similar to what a bank may use, but with fewer hoops and complications—to support our heirs after we are gone. After I am dead, my board is compensated for helping to make financial decisions and allocate money within the parameters of my family bank.

My heirs have the board's support throughout their lives on important financial decisions. They can present business plans to the board and get advice from the experts who support the family trust (both my board and my existing financial team, known as a family office). You can determine your own process in your trust. My family takes annual retreats to build the structure of our trust and prepare the heirs for what we have created.

You get to decide how to handle your trust. When do you want to support your heirs? What do you want to finance or have your heirs use your trust for? You can use their credit scores if you like, or require them to match down payment funds, or give them part of a business loan, but do require that they check in with the board.

## YOUR CASH FLOW BANK

I have whole life, and I use my cash value along the way. It is a great medium-term strategy. It doesn't earn huge rates of return while stored, but it is available when better opportunities arise. The rate on my policies after dividends and net of cost has been between 4% and 5%. One tax-advantaged policy is as high as 6.17%. That's like getting more than 8% in a taxable account, and it's hard to get something at 8% without downside risk.

The cash value doesn't require you to pay tax on dividends that stay in the policy. The first dollars you take from your policy are FIFO: first in, first out. This means it is a return of your premium and you are not required to pay tax. You can also borrow from your cash value. This doesn't impact your credit score (or require you to have a good credit score, for that matter). You can simply use your cash as collateral, and the insurance company will lend you their money. You continue to earn interest, but there is an interest charge from the company in a similar amount. The amount depends on the company, but is usually close to the amount you are currently earning. This avoids any tax, and the payback period is flexible. The loan can also be paid with your death benefit when you die.

The downside risk in whole life comes if you quit early, because there are up-front expenses. If you put money in for a year and then decide you're not going to do it anymore, you'd have been better off in a money market and buying term insurance. But with a properly designed policy, if you put money in for three to five years, you end up ahead. If you do it for between ten and twenty years, the rate of return is between 400% to 800% higher than it would be with a CD or money market—including tax advantages and numerous benefits.

With government-qualified plans like 401(k)s, traditional IRAs, and 403(b)s, the government can change the rules. At one point in the 1990s, they proposed a sundry tax, which meant that if you had more than a certain amount in your retirement account or you pulled more than a certain amount out, you could be hit with an extra 10% tax.

That provision does not exist today, but the government is $30 trillion in debt. What if they need some money to cover those debts? Where are they going to go? They haven't taxed these retirement plans yet (that is, unless you make a distribution) and could easily make a change. But the need for government funding is part of the reason why there's a required minimum distribution when you're seventy-and-a-half. If you don't take it, there's a 50% penalty on what that distribution is supposed to be, plus tax. You could lose a huge amount of that money by not taking it out, but you will be taxed on it when you do. If people hate paying tax now, they hate paying it more when they're older.

If you have a million dollars in a 401(k), that's not a million dollars you can spend. If you take it out before you are fifty-nine-and-a-half, you have to pay taxes on it, along with a 10% penalty. The day you put money in a retirement plan, you are at a 10% disadvantage, yet most feel warm and fuzzy if they have a million dollars in a 401(k). But if you want those million dollars, you can only get around half of it—if you are in the top tax bracket. It's like buying an amazing home but only having keys to half the rooms. That's my problem with these plans, and why I use overfunded cash value as a place to store my money. I can utilize it. When opportunities come, I've got the cash to make moves on them.

## DEFERRING VERSUS SAVING

Deferring tax and saving tax are two different things. *Saving* means you don't have to pay tax. *Deferring* means you don't have to pay tax right now. When people defer, they're not necessarily saving. For example, from 1944 to 1981, the top tax bracket was over 50%. We've had 37.5%

and 39.6% as some of the top brackets over the last several years. What happens if the government starts raising taxes, which it has talked about doing in a substantial way? You might defer tax into a higher tax bracket, where, with your cash value, you could avoid tax through your entire lifetime.

How can you ensure more control over the ever-changing tax landscape? Look for where you can get tax credits, take tax deductions rather than defer, or pay your tax on the seed (up front) rather than on the harvest (in the future). With whole life, you can pay tax now but then have it grow tax-deferred and use strategies to access the funds tax-free.

That, again, is why I like overfunded whole life policies, specifically with mutual companies. If you overfund properly, you minimize the commission to the agent and maximize the cash to you. Even so, of the thousands of companies out there, two dozen at most give you the opportunity to design this properly.

Advisors like Dave Ramsey and Suze Orman, who hate whole life, hate improperly designed whole life first and foremost. But they also hate it for a second reason: they don't understand price versus cost versus value. Again, we are redefining what cheap means in this chapter by dispelling the myth of self-insurance. Dave and Suze think cheap means low payments today, but we want to look at how things work together: the big picture, the tax structure, the risk, and the benefits provided along the way.

It's like buying a car for a dollar versus one for $10,000. You buy the car for a dollar, but if it doesn't run, who cares that it only cost a dollar? The $10,000 car is fully functional. Which one has the higher cost? The one that doesn't run, even though it has a lower price.

All these people look at is the higher initial payment for whole life. But they're not considering the net rate of return on the cash value or the external rate of return due to tax benefits, long-term care benefits (you can access your death benefit while you are alive), disability provisions, and guarantees. Again, only 1.1% of term insurance policies ever pay out. That is fine for short-term protection, but it is a long-term opportunity cost, and I don't like putting my money in something that has a 98.9% chance of failure.

My whole life policy will be around the day I die and come in income tax-free—and likely estate tax-free, due to strategic ownership through a domestic asset protection trust.

## PUAS

I would design whole life to accelerate your cash buildup using paid-up additions (PUAs), which also increase your death benefit. If I start with a $500,000 policy, a base premium that *isn't* overfunded through PUAs grows slowly, takes longer to increase the death benefit, and won't have cash available as quickly. When you use PUAs to overfund, the majority of that cash is available and the death benefit grows. You see an inflection point, especially at around thirteen years. The death benefit starts to grow exponentially versus incrementally, because you've covered the up-front cost of what the insurance companies are required to have in reserves and other costs of doing business, like underwriting and commissions.

The policy that I started out with almost a quarter of a century ago has more than doubled the death benefit today because I funded it at the maximum amount of PUAs without triggering the modified endowment contract (MEC) limit.

## UNIVERSAL LIFE

In the late 1970s and early 1980s, interest rates were high. Mortgages reached a high in 1981 at 16.63%.[15] You could earn double-digit rates on a CD, but you also had to pay tax on those earnings.

At this point, the brokerage E.F. Hutton pioneered universal life, a cash value policy in which the insurance component resembles term, but with a higher cost. Unlike whole life, the cost of universal life insurance is not fixed and can go up over time. In the 1980s, someone could get a small universal life policy, dump a ton of cash into it, and earn high interest rates without having to pay tax on the growth or much insurance cost. There were fewer limits to the amount of money people could put in, so they minimized their insurance and maximized their cash. It was a type of tax shelter during a time of high interest rates. Because the insurance portion was small, there was less risk of rising insurance costs harming the performance of the cash value. But that was before interest rates drastically decreased and the government stepped in with new regulations.

The government was concerned that they were losing too much tax revenue and created lower MEC limits, limiting the amount of cash you could put into such a policy unless you increased your amount of insurance. This increased insurance costs and lowered returns, and the combination of lower interest rates and higher requirements for insurance destroyed the performance of these policies.

The mortality experience—the number of deaths per thousand policy holders—can increase insurance costs, requiring a higher premium or completely consuming the cash value.

With whole life, as I mentioned earlier, your cost of insurance is guaranteed, your premium is guaranteed, you have a minimum guaranteed interest rate, and even your death benefit is guaranteed. Whole life and universal life may seem to have similarities when illustrated, but universal life has fewer guarantees. That doesn't mean there is no place for universal life, but it does mean there are additional risks—and the point is to create certainty, have access to your cash without concern that rising costs might dip into your funds, and know that your death benefit will be around one day longer than you, recapturing your costs like GE did with their pensions and using the cash value for other opportunities as they arise.

## ANOTHER ADVANTAGE TO WHOLE LIFE INSURANCE

When I use this whole life approach, it also provides a rider that is similar to long-term care insurance. If I ever qualify for a nursing home, I can get up to 70% of my death benefit from my whole life contract while I'm alive so I can save on a long-term care premium. With whole life, you don't have to pay for term insurance because you have a death benefit that comes with the overfunded cash value. If you are ever disabled, all of your premium payments will be made by the insurance company after six months, so your savings can still grow and the death benefit will stay intact.

Furthermore, if you are ever sued or go bankrupt, the cash value of your policy is fully protected and can't be touched, unlike money markets, CDs, and savings accounts. Although a retirement plan has protection from liabilities, it often has too much volatility because it's in mutual funds and the stock market.

## WEATHERING FINANCIAL CRISES

Several insurance companies have been around for at least a hundred years and are worth hundreds of billions of dollars. I have a policy with a trillion-dollar company. They have specific restrictions on and requirements for risk management with their funds, which means they have to be relatively stable in order to handle claims.

Crises like the terrorist attacks on September 11, 2001 delivered a big hit to many financial institutions. Insurance companies had death claims to cover, but the companies I had policies with were more stable than the banks I kept money in. Insurance companies cannot fractionalize at the same level as banks. When banks fractionalize, they lend a dollar more than once. When there are defaults, this can have a devastating impact like we saw in 2008.

During the 2008 crisis, a large number of banks went out of business. Others were bought at deep discounts or had to be subsidized by the government to stay afloat. The insurance companies that I hold policies with weren't even close to going out of business.

Some insurance companies do go out of business. Beneficial Life in Salt Lake City didn't make it, but all the policyholders were made whole because it was bought by another insurance company that had to make good on the commitment to those people's contracts.

There are guarantees associated with insurance, just like FDIC for your bank deposits. That said, in my home state, the state guarantee association has never had to pay out a claim (unlike the FDIC). Does that mean that these companies are completely safe? No: economic turmoil can always harm them.

The dividend is not guaranteed until it's paid, but you will get a minimum interest rate of somewhere between 3% and 4.5% before expenses. Once the dividend is paid, if it is, say, 6%, 6% becomes the guaranteed amount for that year (minus expenses). I would only consider companies with at least a hundred-year track record of paying dividends.

## PRICE, COST, AND VALUE

Part of the problem with term insurance is, it phases you out when you have a higher chance of dying. You have a fixed premium for a certain number of years—ten, twenty, or thirty—or sometimes an annually renewable premium that adjusts each year. The longer you guarantee a level premium, the higher the premium is today. If it's annual renewable, you'll probably have the lowest premium today, but over time, it will get exponentially more expensive, especially as you get close to life expectancy. If you hold an annual renewable policy long enough, it could have a higher premium than the death benefit in the later years because they're phasing you out.

With term insurance, the only consideration is price. In order to make a more informed choice, there are two other measurements to consider: cost and value.

Price is what we pay. If you are simply looking at the lowest price today, term is the clear winner. But let's look at cost, which is the net economic impact. Let's say that I have a mutual fund earning 5% net of tax. (This would be low during times of quantitative easing, when the Federal Reserve pours money into Wall Street, but looking long-term, I'll defer to Warren Buffett. He says that if you expect more than 6–7% long-term, you're delusional.)[16] In addition, I have to pay for term insurance, which means I defer some of that money to cover my term. After that cost, I'm getting more like 4.5%. Up front, I'm doing a lot better than the person who buys whole life.

Another problem with most poorly designed whole life policies is that, in the first few years, it feels like that hole I mentioned earlier that you throw your money into: it's all reserves and commission, and no cash value. From a cash comparison perspective, because 90% of companies don't perform well, you're better off buying term and investing the difference.

Nevertheless, there are around two dozen whole life companies that offer properly overfunded policies using PUAs that will have a much higher cash value. That cash value will earn a dividend. Since I started funding my first policy in 1998, my whole life dividends have been much higher than dividends I would earn from savings accounts, money markets, or CDs.

To reiterate an earlier point, as soon as you earn a dividend through whole life, it's guaranteed. Even if the market goes down the next year, you have a minimum guaranteed interest rate cash value, ranging between 3 and 4.5% for most policies. You're now using it as a tax-efficient way to store money without having to wait till age fifty-nine-and-a-half to access it. After three to five years, you'll have more in cash than you deposited. If the policy is designed properly, you could be 400–800% ahead of where you'd be with a money market, CD, or savings account—plus, you have a permanent death benefit. If you take a reduced paid-up policy in the future, you will never make another premium payment, and the death benefit will be guaranteed until the day you die (at a reduced amount). No more premiums will be required for the policy to stay in force.

## USING DEATH BENEFITS

My book *What Would Billionaires Do?* has a chapter titled "Buy Net Worth, Build Cash Flow." In that chapter, I outline six ways you can coordinate your assets to use your death benefit while you're alive, giving you a tax-free asset that provides cash flow. It's a way to unlock lazy or dead assets that don't produce cash flow. Plus, you have cash value that you could use along the way.

I want to reiterate: this is medium-term storage for your money. With runaway inflation, you don't have to leave it sitting in the policy; you can use it to buy assets or pay off high-interest rate loans. One criticism is that whole life doesn't give the best long-term rate of return, and I agree. Nor is it the best short-term option, because money markets and term insurance will be more liquid in the first few years. But between three to five years in, it is a more efficient and protected storage of cash. When interest rates skyrocket, you can pull the cash out and use it for a high-interest account. If interest rates crash, you can store money there until they recover.

I could use my policies to pay off my home tomorrow, if that makes economic sense. I could use them to buy another property. I can pay back the money on my own terms without impacting my credit.

With whole life and PUAs, a very specific strategy has to be appropriately designed in order to function at the level that I'm talking about. The biggest corporations and the wealthiest people, including the Rockefellers, have always used this approach. It isn't for everyone. It's like a hammer: it's no good if you don't know how to use it.

## Chapter Eleven

# Myth 8:
# Debt Is Bad

We're taught by financial pundits to avoid debt like the plague, and on the surface, I agree that it is good to avoid debt. The problem with this pronouncement is the common perception of debt. Most of us are not taught the definition of debt in the true accounting sense; instead, we rely on the common definition of the word, which is anything that is owed to somebody else. But if we don't understand exactly what debt is, how can we effectively avoid it?

People fear debt because they don't understand its technical definition. Understanding the technical definitions of debt and liabilities opens a world of possibility.

| MYTH:<br>Debt is bad, dangerous, and scary. Keep out of it. | REALITY:<br>*Understand the difference between debt and liabilities, and wisely manage and utilize the right liabilities to increase your prosperity.* |
| --- | --- |

## UNDERSTANDING DEBT

An improper understanding of debt is the cause of stress and debate in finance. On my YouTube channel (Garrett.live),[17] there is more opinion and engagement around the topic of debt—especially mortgages—than any other. Most commenters believe that all debt is bad. I agree that it is something to avoid, but most people have the wrong idea about and definition of debt. Debt occurs when you owe more on your loan than the asset attached to the loan is worth. If you borrow to consume with no asset attached to the loan, that creates consumer debt.

### Liability

*Any recurring expense, including many things you may think of as debts, such as mortgages, car loans, small business loans, and so on. The name of the wealth game is not to focus on ridding ourselves of as many liabilities as possible; rather, it is to identify which liabilities are consumptive (take more value from our lives than they add) and which are productive (provide more value than they take), and then focus on increasing our productive liabilities.*

Again, there is a difference between having a loan and being in debt. Debt is a function. It is the relationship of your asset to the liability associated with or attached to that asset. For example, if you have a mortgage of $250,000 but your home is worth $500,000, you do not have debt. Quite the opposite: you have $250,000 in equity. Yet most of the world would tell you that you are $250,000 in debt. With this in mind, how could there be good debt or bad debt? There is no such thing as good debt or bad debt, just debt or no debt.

### Debt

*The state of having more liabilities than assets. Debt is not the same as having liabilities. The only time we are in debt, in the true accounting sense, is when our liabilities are greater than our assets (those things that provide us with income or potential cash flow).*

One of the biggest misconceptions is that all loans are debt, which is not the case. That's right, you can have a loan and be debt-free. Or a loan may be the cause of your debt. So what's the difference? When your asset is worth more than the liability attached to it, you have equity. To call it good debt is both confusing and incorrect.

> **Equity**
>
> *The state of having greater value in assets than in liabilities.*

You see how you can have a loan and *not* be in debt. It all depends on the asset attached to the loan.

When considering debt, the most important question to ask yourself is can your assets create more income than expense? If an asset isn't creating cash flow, then your equity (a.k.a. net worth) may come at a steep cost. An asset has potential value. The difference between that value and what is owed is the equity, or net worth. Net worth is relatively worthless if it can't be converted into cash or, more importantly, cash flow (a.k.a. recurring revenue).

## DOES YOUR LOAN GENERATE POSITIVE CASH FLOW?

Assets come with liabilities. These can be taxes, fees, management costs, or loan payments. A liability is something that creates an ongoing expense. This is why it is essential to understand both your balance sheet and your income statement. The balance sheet is a snapshot of your assets and liabilities. The income statement is a snapshot of your income versus your expenses.

When you have more income than expense, that's called profit. When you have more expense than income, that's called loss. When you have more assets than liabilities, that's called equity. And when you have more liabilities than assets, that's called debt. You can even have more liabilities than assets—debt—and still have a positive cash flow, meaning that those assets are kicking in more income than is needed for the required loan expenses. On the flip side, you can have more expenses than income and still technically have a positive net worth. Do you see how net worth can be deceiving?

To get a more accurate picture of financial health, we should look at the relationship between the balance sheet's assets versus liabilities and the income statement's income versus expenses. Most retirement planning simply looks at net worth or the balance sheet and doesn't really focus on the income statement. This is because retirement planners are focused on the long haul, "set it and forget it" mentality.

If you're not trained to manage and improve your income statement, you might not be as prepared as you could be for retirement.

If your assets do not create cash flow, there may be potential to choose a different asset class, reallocate funds, or simply stop reinvesting and take your cash to build another asset. Look for assets that generate positive cash flow from day one. Doing this requires you to dial in your Investor DNA, to know how to analyze opportunities and manage risk. To minimize risk, it is imperative to have a process for due diligence, the right attorneys and resources, and the ability to navigate different economies. It's easy to make money when times are good, but consider the impact of liabilities during changing markets, downturns, and turbulent economies.

## WHEN LIABILITIES LEAD TO DEBT

A liability can lead to debt. If you borrow to consume or get a loan on a depreciating asset, you can quickly end up owing more than your asset value. Be careful if you borrow to invest (a.k.a. use leverage). Your ability to manage risk and your mindset are two key factors to consider before borrowing money. You've read this far, so you already know that managing risk has to do with your Investor DNA (knowledge regarding the investment), liquidity (access to funds), exit strategy, and the market conditions. Borrowing in times of appreciation may not require much skill to make money, but if the market changes, it may be harder to make payments on the loan.

From 2002 to 2007, I borrowed a lot of money from banks to buy real estate. It was easy to make payments on those loans because I had renters. However, those renters were only covering part of the expense of the liabilities (loans). I didn't think it mattered, because it was a time of high appreciation, and selling some of the properties more than made up for the negative cash flow.

I had 20–100% interest in more than one hundred properties in 2007. The ongoing liabilities associated with my loans were manageable from 2002–2007, but then, in 2008, lending rules changed significantly. Suddenly, the real estate market had a huge supply because investors had bought up houses and homeowners couldn't afford to buy them. Investors didn't have equity and the homes weren't as easy to sell, making it difficult to handle the loan payments. Nor could they get additional loans because lending had come to a halt. They couldn't sell properties because of the depreciating market and were stuck with negative cash flow and, often-times, debt. As investors dumped, foreclosed on, or short-sold properties, an abundance of properties lost significant value. I lost money.

For many real estate investors, these changes were a crushing blow. Many people were financially devastated and felt tremendous guilt about letting their families down. When people get into debt, a common reaction is to feel shame. They don't want people to know about their situation, so they spend too much time alone with their own thoughts and worry. When 2008 hit me hard, I ended up in debt, with lots of mortgages, a change in property value, and negative cash flow. I spent months trying to handle it on my own. *That* mistake cost me millions.

It wasn't until I asked for support that things started to change for my financial and mental well-being.

I remember meeting with my brother-in-law, Derick, who said, "Save money no matter what, even if you are late on a payment. Even at the risk of your credit score." He explained that having savings creates a space for living, for everyday expenses. It also creates a habit.

I also talked with author and mentor Rich Christiansen, who sat down with me for a day and showed me how to refocus and produce. We created a plan that would allow me to devote 75% of my time to the most productive thing I could do to bring in the most cash—teleseminars. I would focus on reaching people and creating value. The other 25% of my time would be spent cleaning up the financial mess.

As I continued to ask for help, one of my coaches, Mark Kamin, advised me to communicate with the banks. Another coach, Norm Westervelt, helped me with those conversations.

Thinking on our own during times of scarcity can keep us stuck. If you are "drowning in debt" or in a precarious financial situation, ask yourself whom you know who can help you. Who can ask better questions? Who can connect you to those who have overcome similar issues?

Eventually, I let go of my embarrassment and negotiated with the banks. In the end, my leveraging mistakes didn't define me. I didn't give up, I asked for help, and I now have new knowledge to help me avoid mistakes along with the ability to manage risk and better weather economic storms.

## THE BENEFITS OF LEVERAGE

Borrowing in times of high inflation has advantages. Over time, your loans will become easier to pay. You use more valuable money up front (the lump sum from the loan) and spread your payments out for years when the dollars are worth less due to inflation. This is great *if* you invest wisely. That can be a big if. Speculating with borrowed money is a recipe for risk, loss, and the creation of bad habits. Before borrowing to invest, make sure you have protected the downside. If leverage causes you to lose sleep or become overly concerned about the long-term viability of the asset you acquire with the loan, remember: the cost of your peace of mind is not worth the potential return.

Most people are not willing to borrow to invest. If the investment loses, you are still on the hook for the loan payment and this creates real debt. If you can cash-flow with the investment or buy the investment when it is worth more than you pay to acquire the asset, you have equity and are using other people's money.

I didn't write much about the downside of borrowing to invest in *Killing Sacred Cows*. If borrowing creates stress on your relationships or your health, or becomes a distraction, it isn't worth it. You are your greatest asset. If scarcity and worry take over, you will be less productive and there is a massive opportunity cost.

I only borrow money when I have money to pay the loan from my liquid assets, like stablecoin or cash value. I am not saying that this is the way everyone else should do it, or that I am the czar of what is right or wrong here. But it is important to create your philosophy. Otherwise, temptations can derail your plan. If you aren't clear about what you want, salespeople will be great at selling you on their plans. Creating your financial methodology takes careful consideration and should be based on your own, individual circumstance. It isn't just about economics; it's about peace of mind.

I only borrow when the rate is lower than my current earnings in savings or investments. Right now, I have a mortgage on my home. The rate is 2.75% and I have cash value dividends that earn 4% or more, depending on when I started the policy. If I wanted to, I could pay off the mortgage next week, but it is more efficient to use my funds for cash value than it is to pay extra toward the mortgage. I have peace of mind around this method and therefore about keeping the mortgage.

Another consideration could be your significant other and how they feel about having a mortgage.

## PAYING OFF LOANS

There are great ways to pay down loans, but it is critical to understand the difference between *method* and *objective*. If you want to pay off your home mortgage as quickly as possible, that is your *objective*. But what is the safest, most efficient *method*? That all depends on your cost of money.

> *If you want to pay off your home mortgage as quickly as possible, that is your objective.*

Cost of money, as I mentioned in Chapter Nine, is the highest net sustainable return you can earn on your dollars. For example, if you are paying 5% on your mortgage but only earning 1% with savings, it may make sense to refinance, make a larger down payment, and start paying extra on your mortgage. In that case, however, you lock your money in equity jail with each payment. In other words, if you want to get that money back from the bank, you will be required to refinance or even take out a second mortgage or home equity line of credit. If there is a place to safely earn 5%, you can automatically save the money, pay the minimum amount to the mortgage, keep control of your funds, and maximize your tax advantages.

People typically make extra payments or shorten their mortgages to save on interest. In order to truly save on interest, though, it is important to realize that we are always paying interest. If we borrow, we pay interest to the bank; if we use our cash, we forfeit the right to earn interest. Both are interest costs. If you aren't sure where to invest or are speculating on the return, paying extra to the mortgage may be the best option, although I encourage you to look for options that leave you with more control of your money before you do.

Now that you've considered objective, let's look at methods. There are multiple ways to pay down loans:

1. **Pay cash.** Few people can pay cash for a home these days. If you do have cash, you may be able to negotiate on price because you can move quickly. I have missed out on properties because I didn't have cash to buy them. And I have acquired properties because I *did* have cash. You want to consider your Investor DNA and your liquidity. Does it make sense to tie your money up in the house? Is it more important to you to have peace of mind because your house is paid off?

2. **Shorten the mortgage.** You could convert your thirty-year mortgage to a fifteen-year mortgage and pay off the loan faster. The reason for this approach is to pay less interest. The downside is, you will have a higher monthly payment and less liquidity because your cash is tied up in equity in your house. Again, ask yourself what matters most to you. Will more cash on hand give you more peace of mind than a mortgage-free home?

3. **Pay extra or make biweekly payments.** By paying extra on your mortgage, you can pay off your loan faster and reduce interest payments. One way to do this is to shift from monthly to biweekly payments. Paying every two weeks, you pay one extra payment per year. This is because there are fifty-two weeks in a year, not forty-eight. Sure, you pay your mortgage off sooner, but that's because you make extra payments, not because it's some magical thing. Again, you could take the extra payments, put that money into an interest-bearing account that earns a rate similar to the rate you're being charged on the mortgage, and keep all your tax benefits, retain control of your money, and still pay off the mortgage early.

4. **Lengthen the mortgage and save the difference.** My preferred method is to lengthen my mortgage to get the lowest monthly payment, save the difference, and control the money. If there's a cash crunch, having more liquidity and lower monthly payments can make all the difference. Note: I always pay at least 20% down in order to avoid PMI (private mortgage insurance).

Investments don't have to look like stocks, bonds, and real estate. If you have loans and don't know what to do with your money, pay off your loans, but do one at a time. Use the cash flow index: take the balance of each loan and divide it by the minimum monthly payment. Pay extra to the one with the lowest number. Pay the minimum amount to every other loan. This will enable you to free up your cash flow in the shortest amount of time.

You could also restructure loans to get better interest rates because rates are low right now. Or you could even reallocate money from volatile or underperforming investments to pay off higher interest loans; that's a guaranteed savings for you. Remember, you can restructure, renegotiate, or reallocate your loans.

For more about debt, including visual examples of balance sheets and income statements, get your free download of *Killing Sacred Cows* at WealthFactory.com/disrupting.

## CREATE MORE VALUE

If we perceive that debt means having liabilities, it can elicit a scarcity mindset filled with fear and worry that minimizes the opportunity to acquire assets. Is it possible to eliminate liabilities from our lives and be productive? I argue that it is not, and this is where the concept of debt goes awry. We do want to avoid true debt—having more liabilities than assets—but we don't want to avoid incurring liabilities that can be beneficial to our productivity, value creation, or prosperity.

Ultimately, the only way to stay out of debt is to create more value in the world than we consume or, in other words, serve more than we are served. This is done by thinking about how we can create value through identifying and fulfilling the wants of others. The net effect of the common advice we hear on debt is the exact opposite of this; the entire focus is on reducing expenses and living in scarcity, rather than focusing on production.

## Chapter Twelve

# Myth 9:
# Financial Security

TRUE FINANCIAL SECURITY DOES NOT COME FROM THE GOVernment, corporations, benefits, or entitlements. It comes from within us. Taking responsibility for our wealth helps us transcend false security and find both true security and freedom.

| MYTH: | REALITY: |
|---|---|
| *Financial security means steady paychecks and benefits. We're entitled to protection and benefits from a corporation, the government, or someone else.* | *We are the only source of security in this life. Unlike those who depend on external forces, we can make ourselves truly secure.* |

## FINANCIAL FREEDOM VERSUS
## ECONOMIC INDEPENDENCE

When you know your Soul Purpose, you will create security. When you know your value, it will be easier for you to create value. Having savings and assets can support you in feeling more financially secure, but your ability to add value, serve people, and solve problems will create lasting security. Making deposits into Relationship Capital means that you will have more people who can support you, thereby creating even more security. The scarcity mindset destroys security by harming our decision-making process and creating a viewpoint that tends to limit value.

Financial freedom and economic independence are both key factors in creating financial security. They are different things. Financial freedom is a state of mind. Financial freedom is when money is longer the primary reason or excuse for doing or not doing something. Money is *a* consideration, but not the *only* consideration. Economic independence, on the other hand, is having enough cash flow to cover your expenses. When you are economically independent, you have a solid foundation and choice in what you do day to day.

Economic independence comes from cash-flowing assets or recurring revenue from a business. What types of investments can you make to bring in ongoing cash flow? Can you create recurring revenue that doesn't require your daily involvement? Real estate, tax liens, hard money lending, dividend-paying stocks, staking stablecoin or other cryptocurrencies—these are all ways to create cash flow.

But what is your Investor DNA? Where do you want to spend your time in order to create economic independence?

Start with your existing resources. Do you have lazy assets? You know, those assets that do not provide cash flow and accumulate instead? Retirement plans, mutual funds, or anything that doesn't create regular, stable cash flow can be converted to cash-flowing assets. Focusing on cash flow, you can create a foundation that, over time, requires less labor from you to pay for your expenses. This will add to your financial security, peace of mind, and financial confidence, and give you the ability to focus on what matters most to you. When you are economically independent and not forced to work, you have more space to do the things you love to do.

You can create economic independence without being a business owner. Not everyone is meant to be an entrepreneur. Building or acquiring companies requires a certain tolerance for uncertainty, and if you do something that isn't aligned with your Investor DNA, you invite risk and destroy financial security.

Business is not the path for everyone, which is good. We don't want a world made up only of entrepreneurs. How would anything ever get done?

It may require different skill sets to run an organization, but with no one to focus on implementation, there would be no organization. You can still implement some of the ideas and strategies geared toward businesses while keeping your job. You might have a conversation with your employer and ask, "If I could create something that adds to the bottom line of this organization, could I participate in a percentage of the upside?" Use resourcefulness and ingenuity to discover ways to increase your income.

Here are some examples of participating in the upside. Years ago, I worked with my team to create a product called "The WealthBook," a book and video player hybrid with nine buttons. Each button allows you to choose different content, including tax strategy, cash flow strategy, and case studies. Each time we sold a WealthBook, my team got a percentage.

There are myriad ways to incorporate this kind of strategy. Another example with my team is they get a percentage of the business from any new strategic relationship they introduce that promotes or supports us.

Some organizations have employee stock option programs (ESOPs), whereby employees can own stock and participate in dividends. Even if you're a W-2 employee, you can do side hustles and use your skills to earn a 1099 income.

## CASH RESERVES AND TURMOIL

My clients Drs. Michael and Torri Gambacorta live in the Carolinas, where there have been devastating hurricanes. After one hurricane, they had to shut down their office and were scrimping to get by. They weren't thinking about or able to help anyone else because they were just trying to survive. Once they recovered, they decided that something had to change, that it was time to be proactive rather than reactive. That is when we started to work together to build savings for a peace-of-mind fund, transfer risk through proper insurance structure, and focus on creating recurring revenue in their business and cash flow with their assets. We did a complete financial health assessment to discover their financial blind spots and what was handled and not handled in their financial plan.

A couple of years later, another devastating hurricane came through. The Gambacortas couldn't open their office for forty-five days, but they had enough cash to get them through. During that time, they were able to think productively because they had more security. Instead of scrambling to survive, they had more resources. Rather than being consumed by fear and uncertainty, they were able to focus on value. Since they couldn't see patients for forty-five days, they created a website, started writing a book, and built a process around a rejuvenating health center. Within six months, they had a monthly income of $100,000 from this center, whereas during the previous hurricane, they were in scarcity, scrambling to survive. This is the difference between scarcity and abundance, proactivity and reactivity. Protecting your mindset is essential to productivity in times that pose the greatest threat, yet create the biggest opportunities.

During the second hurricane, the Gambacortas were in prosperity because they had enough savings. If you don't have at least six months' worth of savings, you're in danger of falling prey to scarcity. We just don't know what will happen when it comes to economic turmoil, the political climate, pandemics, and other major events that blindside most people.

Some people complain that they're not earning any interest on their savings accounts. Maybe not, but they do have an external return. When we have some savings, we have more peace of mind. We can handle short-term turmoil. Rather than scrambling and feeling scared, we can focus on value and productivity—or simply take time to think and regroup as we choose what to do next.

Don't think of your six months' worth of savings as an emergency fund, but a peace-of-mind fund. You don't want to have an emergency to utilize this money. Maybe it is used for opportunity, or simply to protect your mindset. When you have liquidity, you can handle surprises. You have the choice to take some time off, take care of your health or that of a family member, or make a major transition. When you have a peace-of-mind fund or economic independence, you are not beholden to the need to make a dollar tomorrow.

We're all in store for financial surprises, but we can prepare for over 90% of them with the strategies that I'm sharing with you in this book.

## BUILD LIQUIDITY

You've already learned that liquidity—having access to capital or cash—is one important way to protect yourself. When unforeseen circumstances occur, you've got the cash to give you staying power. You don't have to hustle or work an extra job when it's time to focus on the family or yourself and your health.

Have some cash in a safe at home, some cash in the bank, and, potentially, some in cash-value life insurance. Consider storing at least one month's worth of expenses in a digital wallet, in your safe, or on an exchange. You can use stablecoins like USDC, backed by the dollar, and earn interest on exchanges like BlockFi, Nexo.io, Celsius, or Circle. If you want an inflation hedge, you may choose to have some gold or silver in your safe or possibly consider Bitcoin. These will be more volatile than cash, cash value, or stablecoin, so build up at least three months' worth of savings before buying gold or Bitcoin.

You might be wondering, *Where will I get the money I need?* Again, you do this by plugging financial leaks and becoming more efficient with your earnings. You might restructure your loans to lower your payments and allocate the difference to savings. You might cash out underperforming or volatile investments to pay off loans or simply build your savings. Find ways to make more money. How can you create more value to raise your income and increase cash flow and liquidity? How can you utilize untapped resources like Relationship and Mental Capital to bring in revenue?

## THE MOST POWERFUL PROTECTION

The most powerful tool you can use to protect your money and create true financial independence is one people don't often associate with wealth creation: love. You may think it's weird to consider love as it relates to financial security, but hear me out.

Most people think love is dangerous because it makes them feel exposed. But fear actually destroys our protection. When we are afraid, we feel isolated, disconnected, and leery of others. Love is abundantly protective, because it makes people feel confident and supported so that they can live out a vision and do extraordinary and uncomfortable things.

They can make mistakes along the way and still have someone to hug and support them.

Earlier in this book, I mentioned our family retreat in December of 2020. During that time, we had open conversations: "We don't have to go through things alone. We're family. We can share with one another. Worrying isn't helping anyone, so let's just talk about it. What are your worries? Where do you feel burdened?"

Afterward, my dad said, "I feel so much lighter now." We all realized that we have a lot of people who love, care for, and support us. It helped us to feel more confident, make new plans, and commit to growth.

If you died tomorrow, would you have expressed yourself to the people who matter most? Have you communicated the love you have for them? Have you opened up and shared with them so you can heal from what you've been keeping inside? As you heal past trauma and pain, you will feel more secure, more abundant. You will gain confidence and live a life of love.

Where have you held back? Regret and risk come from holding things back, from not asking questions, not being connected. If we censor ourselves for self-protection, we dismantle our humanity.

To whom can you give your whole heart and self? Where do you choose to pour your unconditional love? Choosing love can be a path to discovering more love for yourself and healing from the scarcity thinking that you are not enough—unworthy, unlovable, or lacking value. When you choose love, you can produce more joy, laughter, and value to help people.

At times, people rob themselves of the fulfillment that love brings due to fears of rejection and abandonment. But without love for ourselves, without a feeling of freedom to express the love we have, we lose—and so do the people who love us the most.

When we can let go of the myth that financial security comes solely from money and see that it comes from knowing our value, living our value, and loving, we free ourselves from the fear, doubt, and worry that create scarcity.

# Chapter Thirteen

# BONUS: Cryptocurrency

## BY COREY WERT

A S WE MOVE TOWARD BECOMING A MORE TECHNOLOGI-cally capable society, cryptocurrency—more specifically, its underlying blockchain technology—is poised to become the greatest economic disruption in our history. As you begin to disrupt the sacred cows that have shaped your financial world, it's important that you gain an understanding of this complex topic. My aim in this chapter is not to provide an academic dissertation on cryptocurrency, but rather to offer a general overview of the landscape so you can understand how to both navigate and participate in this incredible opportunity.

In a relatively short period of time, cryptocurrency has moved from the shadows of the dark web and into the mainstream. Corporations have begun to add Bitcoin and other cryptocurrencies to their balance sheets. Innovative companies have quickly adopted blockchain technology as the underpinning of their operations. Even the multitrillion-dollar wealth management industry has changed their tune and opted in by allocating a percentage of their portfolio to this exciting opportunity.

But disruption doesn't go unchecked for long. Increasing interest in cryptocurrency, and adoption of blockchain technology by both institutional and retail parties, has begun to rattle the power centers of society. Countries are racing to establish their own digital dollar. Banks are clamoring to quash decentralized finance through the development of their own centralized blockchains. And governments are working tirelessly to ban or regulate an industry whose founding principle is that it is, in fact, decentralized and unregulated. How this will unfold has yet to be written, but one thing is certain: we are at the precipice of another digital disruption. Blockchain will forever change the world we live in.

## UNDERSTANDING BLOCKCHAIN

To understand the impact of blockchain, let's first draw some parallels to the internet. When the internet was first created, it was primarily a network for academic institutions to share information. At that time, no one anticipated that it would permeate every facet of our lives and completely change the way the world works. It disrupted major industries, leaving those who refused to innovate in the past. E-commerce usurped titans of retail once thought to be untouchable. Streaming services disrupted the media and entertainment landscape. News became immediate. Social media changed the way we connect and interact. And tech companies became the most valuable companies in the world. Today, it's hard to imagine what life would look like without the internet, and those who ventured into this space early made fortunes.

What most people don't realize is that the next great disruption is already on its way—and it is poised to upend the industry once again, arguably on an even larger scale. That disruption is called Web3, and it is powered by blockchain technology.

So, what is blockchain? A blockchain is a database of transactions that is duplicated and distributed across the entire network of computer systems on the blockchain. This decentralized database, managed by multiple participants, is known as distributed ledger technology (DLT), an open-source ledger that creates complete transparency in an economic system.

One key difference between a typical database and a blockchain is in how the data is structured. A blockchain collects information together in groups, known as blocks. Each block in the chain contains a number of transactions, and every time a new transaction occurs in the blockchain, a record of that transaction is added to every participant's ledger.

Blocks have certain storage capacities and, when filled, are closed and linked to the previously filled block, forming a chain of data known as the blockchain. Each block is given an exact time stamp when it is added to the chain. All new information that follows that freshly added block is compiled into a newly formed block, which will also be added to the chain once it is filled.

This data structure creates an inherently irreversible timeline of data when implemented in a decentralized fashion—meaning that, if one block in one chain was hacked and changed, it would be immediately apparent that it had been tampered with. Unlike traditional databases, this method of stringing blocks together creates a system of recording information that makes it difficult to change the information or cheat the system. If hackers wanted to corrupt a blockchain system, they would have to change every block in the chain, across every distributed version of the chain.

The goal of blockchain is to allow digital information to be recorded and distributed, but not edited. In this way, a blockchain is the foundation for transactional records that cannot be altered, deleted, or destroyed. Blockchains are constantly and continually growing as blocks are added to the chain, which significantly adds to the security of the ledger. The disruptive innovation of a blockchain is that it guarantees the fidelity and security of a record of data and generates trust without the need for a trusted third party.

For example, in the case of DeFi, a peer-to-peer financial instrument built on blockchain, it is possible to move funds between two parties without need for a third-party intermediary such as a bank. In a typical financial transaction, there is a lot of friction. The bank needs to verify that the sender has the funds, there is a system to transfer the funds, and another intermediary needs to validate receipt of the funds. Through the use of smart contracts and the distributed ledger system, DeFi eliminates the need for financial institutions to act as intermediaries and validate each step of the process. The end results of the blockchain solution are operational simplification, reduced fees, automated compliance, and faster settlements.

While blockchains are best known for their crucial role in systems such as DeFi, their application is growing. Another strong case for blockchain is within the real estate industry. Real estate has been rampant with fraud for centuries, ranging from people selling properties they don't own to banks giving out questionable loans. The 2008 housing crisis, which led to the 2009 economic recession, was the catalyst that gave birth to Bitcoin that same year.

The real estate industry also requires involvement from several third parties to finalize a transaction: attorneys, title companies, and banks or mortgage companies. With cryptocurrency and blockchain technology, smart contracts are programmed into an asset itself, eliminating the need for an attorney. The open-source ledger at the heart of blockchain allows the buyer to verify the seller's ownership, eliminating the need for a title company. That same ledger allows the seller to verify the buyer's funds, eliminating the need for an escrow account. You can even eliminate the need for a bank or mortgage company, as loans can come from cryptocurrency loan pools. All in all, executing a real estate transaction through blockchain can speed up the transaction, reduce the risk of fraud, and significantly reduce cost.

These are just two examples. The potential of blockchain has many applications and is set to disrupt major industries, bodies, and practices, including travel and transportation; manufacturing and supply chain management; commerce; media and entertainment; telecommunications; cybersecurity; networking and the internet of things; healthcare and insurance; the law and government; philanthropy and voting. Imagine a fully transparent voting system that keeps immutable records and still retains voter anonymity.

## HOW ARE CRYPTOCURRENCIES CREATED?

So, now that we have established what blockchains are, how do you find your investment opportunity within these systems and the cryptocurrencies that fund them? First, let's draw some parallels between the crypto market and the traditional stock market so you can understand how cryptocurrencies are issued.

When a company starts to grow in a traditional market, it needs capital to sustain that growth and will usually seek out private investment, in exchange for stock, to fund the expansion. In many cases, this happens first through venture capital. Venture capital (VC) is a form of private equity, a type of financing in which investors provide start-up companies or small businesses that are believed to have long-term growth potential with much-needed capital to hire employees, build infrastructure, and begin marketing on a much larger scale. This capital is typically first raised through VC firms, investment banks, and other financial institutions that act as early investors. Sometimes a company may opt to go public to raise more money through an initial public offering (IPO), in which the company issues stocks to the general public.

When a blockchain company wants to raise capital, they do so through an initial coin offering, or ICO. ICOs are similar to IPOs in that they both mark the first time the general public can purchase the "coin" or stock in the hopes of getting in early and benefiting as it appreciates in value.

The idea behind an ICO is similar to an IPO, but the process differs quite a bit. Whereas an IPO is highly standardized and regulated, an ICO is somewhat of a do-it-yourself process. The team behind the project outlines their plan in a white paper for the new system, explaining what it is and how it works. That is normally followed by a marketing plan to raise awareness and draw in investment. At this stage—similar to the private investment stage—coins are made available as a pre-ICO. During this period, the company will issue coins, normally at a discounted rate, to raise the funds they need to continue building out the project. From there, they can try to get listed on an exchange such as Binance, Coinbase, or Robinhood to gain broader exposure and draw in more capital investment from the general public. This is, of course, a simplistic overview of how an ICO works to give you an idea of how a cryptocurrency is created and launched. The process can be much more complex.

While both IPOs and ICOs share the same goal, which is to raise funds from the public, there are a few key differences. IPO valuations reflect careful and thorough research into a company's books and performance, whereas an ICO does not and relies heavily on hype and investor sentiment. The process of an ICO is unregulated, so you have to be careful. The crypto market can provide mind-boggling returns; thus, it attracts greed, which in turn attracts scammers. There are numerous examples of "rug pulls" in which blockchain companies lure in investors only to disappear with the funds. If you are going to participate in the early stage of a project, you need to do your research and due diligence.

Another way to accumulate coins, outside of buying them on exchanges, is through the process of mining. Any cryptocurrency that uses the proof-of-work (PoW) consensus model can be mined. Cryptocurrencies that use other consensus models, like proof-of-stake (PoS), cannot be mined and can only be acquired through purchase.

To explain mining, let's use Bitcoin, which uses a proof-of-work (PoW) model. Bitcoin mining is the process by which new Bitcoins are entered into circulation. It's also the method with which the network confirms and verifies new transactions, which is why it's called PoW, and is therefore a critical component of the blockchain's ledger maintenance, development, and security. Miners provide computational power to the network with the aim of solving extremely complex mathematical equations. The first computer to find the solution mints the block and is awarded the Bitcoins associated with that block. Miners then sell those coins on exchanges to recoup the cost of running their mining networks.

The number of Bitcoins awarded in each block changes over time. After every 210,000 blocks have been mined, there is a "halving event." When this happens, the number of Bitcoins awarded per block is reduced by half. This was an intentional feature in Bitcoin's software to reduce the coins' rate of inflation.

In the early days, the mining process could be performed using a laptop, but today, the process requires sophisticated hardware. You also compete against companies with massive server farms that run indefinitely to provide them as much computational power as possible and increase their likelihood of finding and minting the block.

While I believe that mining is no longer a viable opportunity for the average person, it is an important concept to explain so you can understand how coins are created for projects using the PoW model. Many projects are moving away from that model, as it is energy-intensive and the industry is looking for a more sustainable, environmentally-friendly solution, such as PoS (Proof of Stake).

## CRYPTOCURRENCIES AND INVESTOR DNA

So how do you find your investment opportunity in this industry? As Garrett mentions often, it's important to know your Investor DNA. There are ample opportunities in the crypto universe, with over 10,000 cryptocurrencies in existence. You also have multiple markets to choose from: DeFi, non-fungible tokens (NFTs), meme coins, gaming, and the metaverse, to name but a few.

Just as when you invest in traditional markets, it's imperative that you determine the risk and build your plan. I recommend only investing in areas that you know or are willing to learn.

Is there money to be made in real estate? Yes. Is there money to be made in the financial markets? Yes. Is there money to be made by investing in yourself and creating something? Yes. But if you spread yourself too thin or move blindly into something you don't know, it will most likely end in disaster.

Because this is the early days of cryptocurrency and, in my opinion, similar to the internet bubble of the 1990s, there is a lot of excitement in this space. However, I know that not all projects will survive. To decide whether you should invest in cryptocurrency, you first need to decide if it fits your Investor DNA.

There are several things I look at before investing in a project so it fits my Investor DNA: real-world utility, proven use case, a great leadership team, the maximum supply of coins, and a clear roadmap for development.

As I mentioned above, I view the world of blockchain, and thus cryptocurrency, as the next phase in our digital evolution. But unlike the move from an analog world to a digital one—in which entirely new user behavior was being created and impossible to predict—in this next evolution of Web2 to Web3, we have a trail of breadcrumbs to follow. We can look back and see what advancements gained global adoption and find companies innovating in that space through the advancement of blockchain. Here are a few examples of projects that are doing exactly that. (This is not investment or financial advice; it is for educational purposes, to illustrate my point.)

Theta is a blockchain-powered project that provides video streaming services (think Netflix). The developers of the project aim to shake up the current state of the video streaming industry. In the current environment, centralization and high costs mean that end users often have a poor or expensive experience. Content creators earn less revenue due to the barriers between them and end users, with the vast majority of profits going to the third-party intermediary. This project more closely connects creators with end users. Samsung and Theta entered into a partnership that could see Theta.tv included as a native app in Samsung devices. This partnership would get Theta in front of millions of households worldwide, and the resulting benefit to investors in Theta could be enormous.

Filecoin is a decentralized, blockchain-powered storage system. The project aims to disrupt the cloud storage industry. Unlike cloud storage companies that are centralized, meaning that your data is owned by those companies, the decentralized nature of Filecoin aims to allow people to be the custodians of their own data, making the web more accessible and harder to censor.

Syntropy is a project that aims to decentralize and solve the many issues prevalent in the current internet framework, including security, privacy, governance, and performance. They are building a better, and more private, internet in every possible way.

Vechain is a project that innovates in the supply chain and logistics industry, an industry that hasn't seen significant innovation in decades. They have been able to demonstrate massively boosted efficiency, traceability, and transparency across data trails within supply chains. Because of this, their client list is growing quickly and already includes the likes of Starbucks, BMW, and McDonald's.

The Graph is a project that is creating an indexing protocol for querying data across the blockchain networks that power many of the DeFi and Web3 ecosystems (think Google). Vitalik Buterin, the creator of Ethereum, has even gone on record saying that this is his favorite project because he sees the utility it will provide as the blockchain ecosystem continues to expand.

Are the blockchain projects I mentioned above guaranteed to win? No. Google wasn't the first search engine. Facebook wasn't the first social media platform. Who knows if another company will come along with a better mousetrap and take over the market. But as I look at the horizon over the next five to ten years, what I do like about the premise of these projects is that they are focused on innovating in services that have already garnered widespread user adoption. I also appreciate that they are looking to disrupt industries with billion- or trillion-dollar revenues.

In addition to choosing projects that fit my Investor DNA and that I am willing to invest in, I also avoid investing in markets I don't want to participate in or support—for example, the metaverse. The metaverse is a rare example of something entirely new that will shape new societal behavior. Just as the internet transformed our access to information, and social media changed the way we connect, it's inevitable that the metaverse will become a massive industry as it creeps into our everyday lives. Facebook sees this opportunity and has rebranded to Meta. Top apparel and luxury brands are buying "land" and developing metaverse properties. In fact, the first mortgage was recently issued for a plot of digital land in one of the leading platforms, Decentraland. The metaverse is going to create an entirely new digital commerce, and I can see how it will become a part of everyday life at some point. However, I believe the metaverse, if used irresponsibly, to be harmful to society and social connection. It's one more layer further removed from reality. Therefore, I choose to opt out with my dollars and not participate. Will riches be made in this market? Yes. But it's not the only opportunity, and I choose to invest in technologies that push us forward as a society, not set us back.

## ASSESSING PRICE POTENTIAL

After identifying a project that fits with my Investor DNA, I like to use a simple equation to determine the "price potential" of a coin. Of course, a lot goes into the forecast of the actual market price of an asset: the order book; market dynamics; the news cycle; social sentiment; and, within the crypto universe, oddly enough, a tweet from Elon Musk. So when I talk about assessing price potential, I am not trying to forecast what the market price will be today, tomorrow, or next week. I am simply looking at a coin's potential.

To illustrate this point, let's use Bitcoin. Bitcoin has a relatively small and finite supply. It was programmed to mint a maximum of twenty-one million coins, with experts forecasting that the last coin will be minted in the year 2140. The actual number of coins that will be in circulation after all coins are minted is forecasted to be closer to eighteen million, since coins have been lost over time as people lose access to the digital wallets or hard drives where their coins are stored. As of this writing, roughly nineteen million coins have been minted.

To assess the "price potential" of Bitcoin, all we have to do is use a simple economic model of supply and demand. If demand for the asset increases at a rate faster than supply is added to the market, the price moves up. This is why we've seen the increased demand for Bitcoin in the last few years push its price to incredible highs. Conversely, if the supply of Bitcoin increased at a rate that outpaced demand, those inflationary measures would suppress the price. As the minting of new coins will continue to decline rapidly—with the remaining two million coins being added to the supply over the next 120 years—if demand continues, the current price of Bitcoin has not even begun to test its potential.

Here's the equation I use to determine the "potential" price of cryptocurrency:

### PRICE = MARKET CAP ÷ CIRCULATING SUPPLY

If the market cap of a project increases—meaning that demand increases and dollars pour into the project—and circulating supply remains static, the price will go up. If the market cap remains static and the circulating supply goes up—meaning that more coins are minted and added to the circulating supply—the price will decline. It's a simple hypothesis and, on a macro scale, incredibly effective for estimating the price potential of a coin. If you've ever wondered why some coins are worth thousands or tens of thousands while others are worth pennies or fractions of a penny, this equation is the reason. You cannot assess the price potential of a coin without understanding the simple fundamentals of market cap and supply.

Let me use another example to illustrate this point. In 2021, a project called Dogecoin witnessed incredible growth over a two-month period as it appreciated in price from roughly five cents to seventy cents, creating millionaires along the way.

Dogecoin is a meme coin. Its price is driven primarily by speculation and social sentiment rather than utility. In 2017, the creators of the project launched it as a joke. Their intention was to poke fun at the wild speculation in cryptocurrencies at a time when the industry was gaining attention and broad retail interest was pouring into the market. This sent prices on a historic run before a massive, market-wide correction in December of the same year.

When the price of Dogecoin ran from five cents to seventy cents in 2021, posting a 1400% return, the creators of the project had abandoned it and were no longer supporting its development. The price run was part of a larger market sentiment, but what really drove up the price was a tweet from Elon Musk, declaring that it was his favorite coin. This led investors to pour their dollars in.

During this time, Garrett and I held a mastermind. The night before, Dogecoin had doubled in value. I asked the mastermind attendees how many of them owned Dogecoin. Several people raised their hands. After jokingly suggesting that they leave the mastermind immediately, I encouraged them to sell and take a profit. During the breaks, several people came up to me and asked why I would say this. They were puzzled because they firmly believed that it could go to one dollar. One attendee even tried to convince me that it would go to ten dollars. This prompted me to build a scenario using my simple equation to illustrate what it would take for Dogecoin to reach ten dollars, and how unlikely that was.

At the time of the analysis, Dogecoin had a circulating supply of roughly 130 billion coins in circulation.

If

**PRICE = MARKET CAP ÷ CIRCULATING SUPPLY**

then it is also true that

**MARKET CAP = PRICE × CIRCULATING SUPPLY**

Therefore, using a price of ten dollars,

**$1,300,000,000,000 = 10 × 130,000,000,000**

For Dogecoin to reach ten dollars, the market cap would have to reach $1.3 trillion. That's $1.3 trillion for a meme coin with little utility or real-world value. And that's if it stopped increasing its supply. At the time of my analysis, Dogecoin was issuing nearly 14.5 million coins per day. To put this in perspective, a market cap value of this magnitude would have made Dogecoin the sixth largest company in the world, falling between Google and Facebook.

When coins start to "moon," it's easy for investors to lose perspective in the flurry of absurd price predictions they find on Crypto Twitter and YouTube. Greed and FOMO set in, which leads to poor decision-making and, ultimately, losses.

I use the above equation almost every day when looking at potential investments. There is a wide variety of apps that can provide you with all the info you need to run your own analysis. Hopefully, this simple equation can put things into perspective and help you assess the price potential of a coin when evaluating your investment opportunity.

## IN CONCLUSION

To capitalize on this incredible opportunity, it's important to identify your investor DNA. Pick your market, identify projects that provide real-world utility, and do your due diligence. Keep your feet on the ground and trust the fundamentals. The volatility of the market is not for the faint of heart, but with due diligence, the rewards could be well worth it.

Though we don't know exactly what is in store as blockchain and cryptocurrency continue to mature and transform industry, we can be certain that we are on the cusp of another great disruption. Blockchain will revolutionize the way the world works, and the cryptocurrency market represents one of the greatest wealth-generation opportunities of our lifetime. In it's short history, Bitcoin alone has already created 100,000 millionaires.[18]

With these numbers in mind, it's easy to think you have missed the opportunity. A tremendous amount of wealth has been accumulated by the early adopters of this industry, but we are still in the infancy of this disruption. At the time of this writing, less than 5% of the world's population owns any form of cryptocurrency. As the saying goes, the best time to plant a tree was twenty years ago; the next best time is today.

# Chapter Fourteen

# Create a Game Worth Winning

IN THE SUMMER OF 2017, I DID SOMETHING OUT OF THE ORDI-nary, something I hadn't thought was possible. I'd had the idea for a long time, but it was accompanied by a constant, nagging doubt. Imagining taking this step was exciting but uncomfortable.

Though I had kept it a secret, this idea had been on my mind since I was eighteen. I was surprised when my wife, Carrie, asked me, "Do you want to spend the summer in Italy as a family?"

Somehow, she knew my secret wish. I guess I shouldn't have been surprised, because she knows me better than anyone else.

Carrie painted a picture of our family really connecting and having fun, immersing ourselves in another culture, seeing where my family came from, and growing together before the kids left the house.

When we first spoke about spending the summer in Italy, it seemed like a far-off, impossible dream. Preparing for it meant more than buying tickets and reserving a place to stay. To make this trip happen, I had to confront fears and break the invisible chains that had held my family back for generations.

As a business owner, I was uncertain about how I could take a sum-mer off. I had employees. I was the primary speaker at our events. Those challenges were solvable, but the real issues holding me back were subtler and much harder to admit and address.

My father and grandfathers were all hardworking coal miners, so a summer trip of leisure, sightseeing, and wine tastings on another continent was something that had never been done or even considered in my family before. Quite frankly, it seemed like a ridiculous idea, out of reach, unlikely, and, well, even scary.

Money always felt scarce in my family. This makes sense when you consider the path they took to come to America and how they earned their living. You might remember the short story about my great-grandfather Biagio Iaquinta, which I shared in Chapter One. He was born in a small town in southern Italy and had never been able to afford to see even the great cities in his own country. With his very survival constantly at stake, there was no time for recreation or relaxation.

In the early 1900s, he was struggling to make a living in San Giovanni in Fiore, Italy, and barely able to feed his family. When entrepreneurs today say they have to put food on the table, they are using a metaphor as an excuse for workaholism (a type of escapism), but my great-grandfather faced this challenge daily as an actual, stark, and terrifying reality.

He somehow managed to scrape together enough money to sail to America with his father, brother, and half-brother, but had to leave his pregnant wife behind. It took weeks to hike to the nearest port through the mountains of southern Italy, and they barely survived the sea voyage; their only source of sustenance was "honey bread," which gets hard and doesn't mold. Their ship finally docked at Ellis Island on November 4, 1913.

Two of the three Iaquintas did not speak a word of English. The only people they knew were some Italians and Greeks working the coal mines in central Utah, so as soon as they were able, they slowly made their way west once again—this time by train—and finally arrived at what must have felt like the other side of the world, thousands of miles from anything they knew.

Once in Utah, they learned that a terrible mining disaster had recently occurred, limiting the number of available jobs. Biagio started herding goats and sheep. He did this for years until, eventually, he was hired by another coal mine.

My great-grandfather was separated from his family and felt a deep and constant sense of economic insecurity. Work in the mines could be unpredictable and inconsistent because of shutdowns, disasters, and strikes, but he was willing to do whatever it took for his family to join him. So, despite barely making enough to survive, he scrimped and saved every penny, sending whatever he could back to his wife in Italy.

He was so poor that he even lived in a tent for years until he managed to save enough money to secure a house and finally afford to bring his wife and child—the now seven-year-old daughter he'd never met—to America.

It is hard to fathom being separated from family for more than seven years. I can't imagine what it must have been like for Biagio to miss the birth and early childhood of his daughter, cross an ocean with little food, navigate a new country without speaking the language, or survive back-breaking work when the only place he had to come home to was a dirty tent.

The overwhelming poverty Biagio experienced affected his mind so deeply, it created a framework of scarcity so powerful that it was handed down for generations and greatly influenced the Italian side of the family's money management philosophy. For example, his daughter, my great-aunt, buried coffee cans filled with money in her backyard and hoarded more toilet paper than she could ever use. My grandfather's cellar was literally filled with rolled-up bills, just tucked away in corners and crevices.

This extreme level of saving and hoarding is caused by the scarcity, worry, and fear that come from such extreme life situations, and a circum-stance-induced scarcity mindset can be passed down through stories and family anecdotes that become legends, instilling doubt for generations to come.

Even though my great-grandfather died while I was still a baby, his fear, scarcity, and hardships permeated my life through family stories and philosophies. Scarcity can limit vision, cloud the future, and hold people captive.

The idea that we must hold on to what we have because there may not be enough, or that a lack of money can separate us from our loved ones, can be debilitating. These circumstances created a way of life for my family that was governed by scrimping, saving, and sacrificing. Yes, sacrificing. But the question became, when do we stop sacrificing? When will the struggle end?

In my family, sacrifice was all we knew. It was how we operated; it became our way of being. But fortunately, there was a glimpse of hope, and I was shown a different way.

Much of my drive and passion comes from my hero, Biagio's son—my grandfather, James Anthony Eaquinto. (Our family name, like many others, was changed when Biagio landed on Ellis Island).

James grew up in East Carbon, Utah and was a full-time coal miner. Although the fear of scarcity inherited from his father kept him in the coal mines, he also found time to run a TV sales and repair shop. On the weekends, he toured with his band, playing the accordion. His example was enough to plant a seed of possibility for me. He showed me that I could choose to do something enjoyable on my own terms rather than work only for money. That I didn't have to be held captive by a fear of money. That I didn't have to risk my life for a paycheck or allow my past to dictate what is possible (or impossible) for me. That a life of value could replace a life of scarcity.

With his "side hustles," my grandfather became respected in his community. I saw this firsthand when I rode along with him on TV repair calls. His customers gave him appreciation, praise, and even gifts. I remember someone making homemade tamales and enchiladas for him. He won the Community Person of the Year Award. He even helped to build parks and do other things to improve his small town. He was the glue of our family and did whatever he needed to support his community.

My grandfather's example gave me just enough courage to finally break the mold. He inspired me to start my own business as a teenager and gave me all the support and encouragement I needed.

My very first official business, which I started when I was fifteen, was "Garrett Gunderson's Car Care," a relatively low-risk endeavor, but when I graduated college and wanted to start a more serious venture, this was concerning, even frightening, to my family. They wanted to know about the risks.

"What about job security?"

"What happens if it doesn't work out?"

"What will you do if there's no money coming in?"

My family didn't see me starting a financial business as "a real job" and was concerned about my path. My grandfather saw entrepreneurship as potentially risky and something to do on the side. He loved me and had the best intentions, but his fear and perspective created massive conflict for me because I didn't want to disappoint him.

After graduating college, I was offered about a dozen jobs, but none of them truly called to me. Even though my professors and family thought they were amazing, stable companies at the time, places like Merrill Lynch, Strong Investments, Inc., and Arthur Andersen, all of which made great offers, aren't even around anymore.

My family felt I should take one of these jobs because their perspective was formed by trauma experienced generations ago. The trauma haunted us like whispers from the dark waves of the ocean my great-grandfather crossed decades before, or the nightmares that accompanied years of cold nights all alone in his tent, without his family.

Trauma leaves a shadow of doubt, a fear of worst-case scenarios like being separated from family or losing what has come at such a steep cost.

My great-grandfather Biagio was bold, but his boldness came with a price, considering that he had to leave his family for years to start something new. He sacrificed and risked so much, missing out on memories as he worked to create economic security and keep the family together.

It was the beginning of a legacy. And now it was my turn to create a new, true, and lasting legacy by making the next move. Following my own career path was one of my first experiences with doing something uncomfortable or out of the ordinary, and with choosing Soul Purpose over perceived security.

The reality is that the only true security we experience comes from choosing Soul Purpose. It doesn't exist in a bank account, or even a job. It exists in value creation, relationships, and doing what we do best.

To find security, I had to make the difficult decision to start a business. Within the first few months after my graduation, my business had a six-figure month when an early mentor became a client. The first person I showed my accounts to was my grandfather, James. I wasn't bragging; I just wanted him to know that I would be okay, that it was working.

He was proud. He looked me in the eye, put his hand on my shoulder, and teared up when speaking these very words: "I. Am. Proud." He wanted what was best for me, and that required that I rewrite our family history by breaking through scarcity.

Despite his initial concerns, my grandfather supported me. He even invested both time and money in me by becoming my first client. I could feel that my choice was changing our family's financial destiny, our future, our legacy.

Still, it wasn't easy to confront the fears. My family wanted what was best for me but didn't always know what that was. And because I was going down a new path at the time, I didn't know either. My journey was about inventing a new future, following a different formula, even having a career that went beyond trading time for money. I didn't know it at the time, but it was also about honoring my ancestors by living my Soul Purpose, taking the best from our lineage and embracing those ideas, and finally, truly letting go of the scarcity and fear. Letting go of the fear didn't mean letting go of family, it meant honoring and loving them, and loving myself.

By choosing to invent what I want to do for a living (educator, writer, comedian), I have changed the course for future generations. I'm doing something that matters—something I love, that excites me and utilizes my gifts. I choose to live a fulfilled life with family, love, passion, and Soul Purpose at the center. Sometimes a bold move, where you lead by example, can change your family destiny forever.

But the remnants of scarcity that prevented my grandfather from ever visiting Italy were still alive in me. I had made progress in my career, but there was still more to overcome to create a life I didn't want to retire from. I had to let go of the myth that my livelihood, my wealth, was tied to physically being at work. And I had to let go of the fear that taking time to just be with my family was a luxury I could never afford, no matter how much money I accumulated.

Fear can hold people captive. It can show up as worry and doubt or despair and difficulty. This can become a script for generations, but only if you allow it to happen.

It is hard to find our Soul Purpose in a script of fear and the noise of the world. When we're caught up in the trappings and pain of the past, our Soul Purpose is lost and our voice is drowned out. Doubt is deafening and worry is a relentless villain. The narratives we come from, false narratives of what is "possible" or "impossible," can have debilitating echoes.

But what is impossible to one person may be exciting and completely possible to another. People can't understand or define your Soul Purpose because it is different from theirs. Possibility comes from within you, from your willingness to listen to yourself and your intuition rather than believe the lies of scarcity or fear. You are not destined for the same circumstances as those who came before you, nor do you have to be defined by their fear.

You can be bold.

You can choose your own adventure, write your own destiny.

My grandfather loved everything about Italy. My family showed love through food and used recipes handed down by their ancestors. My grandfather knew the traditions and felt the pride of being Italian; he talked about the old country, but never from experience, since he couldn't break the chains of scarcity to ever make it there.

Just like starting a business and breaking the mold, a winning game or dream begins with an idea.

"Let's go to Italy for the summer."

This was the game, the idea.

Even if you don't think you have the power or resources to realize a dream in the moment, you can speak it into existence by being bold enough to consider it.

In 2017, my family and I returned to the country where my family's story began. We rented a villa in Tuscany for two months and hired a maid and a private chef. This game began with a conversation with my wife and ended up changing my entire life.

We found a way to speak going to Italy into existence. Then we booked a flight. Carved out the time on the calendar. Rented the villa. Invited friends and family. It was the first time in our marriage that my wife and I were together for sixty-three straight days with no business trips, no interruptions.

We also got to experience the best Italy has to offer—Siena, Verona, Venice, Rome, restaurants, art. We've come full circle, from an impoverished Italian family barely scraping by to an American family that can travel to Italy or anywhere else in the world we want to by disrupting sacred cows.

My great-grandfather's mission was survival. But he created the conditions for me to thrive personally and the opportunity for me to live a life that I love. That is my great-grandfather's legacy, and now it is mine.

Speaking something into existence happens in a single moment—a single shift in thinking. It begins with a thought, an idea. If you are bold enough to speak it into existence, you can write a new chapter in your book of life. You are the author. Your pen is the key. Write it, speak it, live it. What will you choose?

# Resources and Self-Study for Overcoming Scarcity, Healing Childhood Trauma, and Processing Pain

I N THIS BOOK, I STICK TO MY AREA OF EXPERTISE: MONEY. BUT when I wrote *Killing Sacred Cows,* I had little idea of the connection between our childhoods and our current views on and relationships with money.

So, how do you heal? What is next for you? I include books, websites, people, and more in this list with the hope that at least one of these resources will resonate with you and unlock your gifts and life, too.

## BOOKS AND ARTICLES

Okay, I have to admit, I haven't read as much on this topic due to time spent working directly with therapists, health practitioners, and gifted healers. I act quickly, while my wife is more of a researcher. Many of these books are recommended by the practitioners who helped me. They may help you discover your own path of healing.

Hiking with my friend Joe Polish one day, I told him about how stiff and painful my neck was. He commented that it was probably psychosomatic and referred me to *The Great Pain Deception: Faulty Medical Advice Is Making Us Worse* by Steven Ray Ozanich. After reading the first chapter, I had Joe connect me with the author for a Skype call. I mean, it made sense: pain in the neck. It's something we say all the time, and it had manifested for me. One session and my pain started to release, and my neck hasn't gone out in years.

My wife loves the book *What Happened to You? Conversations on Trauma, Resilience, and Healing* by Bruce D. Perry, MD, PhD and Oprah Winfrey. We use the methodology in the book as parents and believe that it will be instrumental in how our kids process and heal from pain and trauma.

One of my therapists, Annie King, recommends *The Body Keeps the Score: Brain, Mind, and Body in the Healing of Trauma* by Bessel van der Kolk. I haven't read the book, but I have used Kolk's techniques to release the physical pain stored in my body due to unprocessed mental and emotional pain. In one session, I was able to move my shoulder for the first time in a month. Before that session, I had tried stem cells, dry needling, PRP and prolozone injections, physical therapy, and, well, just about everything. If you are feeling physical pain and have emotional trauma in your life or don't remember your childhood, you may want to read this.

*How to Change Your Mind: What the New Science of Psychedelics Teaches Us About Consciousness, Dying, Addiction, Depression, and Transcendence* by Michael Pollan is a book I bought and started to read; then someone borrowed it and I lost track of it. But I have seen Pollan in documentaries and have had so many friends read and recommend the book that I think it could be useful.

*The Biology of Belief: Unleashing the Power of Consciousness, Matter & Miracles* by Bruce H. Lipton, PhD has been at the center of countless conversations I have had with colleagues, friends, and mentors. This book gives insight into the impact our vision can have on us at a cellular, biological level. Eye-opening and simply brilliant.

*Love and Loving* by Jim Gordon is a seminal work that led me to meditation and the path of sound and light.

*When the Body Says No: The Cost of Hidden Stress* by Gabor Maté is another book that many of the people I work with recommend. I have watched videos with Maté and love the insights.

One of the quickest and most effective ways to learn about MDMA therapy is from my friend Tucker Max and his amazing article, "What MDMA Therapy Did for Me," which you can find on Medium.com.

## WEBSITES AND DOCUMENTARIES

The website I visit most often to listen to talks and podcasts is ILM.org. When I met the founders of Inner Light Ministries (ILM), it was an experience of unconditional love. They weren't interested in what I could do for them or my public persona, they simply treated me with love, the way they treat everyone else they come into contact with. This has been the most foundational, integral, and instrumental resource in my life.

When my son Breck was young, we took him to Disneyland. At the pool, another child bumped into him by the slide, and he cracked his head open on the ground. We rushed him to the hospital, where he was scared and eventually put into a straitjacket by three doctors in masks so they could stitch up his head. This created a fear of anyone in a mask—mascots, the Easter Bunny, etc. This fear consumed him for years until we were referred to EMDR, another great resource for handling and healing trauma. It worked amazingly, and he is fully healed from this traumatic event. Go to EMDR.com to learn more.

Almost twenty years ago, a financial mentor of mine, Vince D'Addona, recommended that I attend the Landmark Forum. There, I was able to pinpoint three times in my childhood that negatively shaped my behavior and beliefs. Working with Landmark also allowed me to see the mask that I was hiding behind that prevented me from fully connecting and being present. Landmark is relatively inexpensive, but in exchange, you get upsells to other courses. Go to LandmarkWorldwide.com to learn more.

As far as using psilocybin as part of therapy, check out the Psychedelic Somatic Institute and read their white paper at PsychedelicSomatic.org.

I also recommend viewing the documentary *Fantastic Fungi* for more information.

## PEOPLE

It is hard for me to express exactly what Teri Cochrane does, but it is nothing short of magical; she is a gift. I have referred so many people who consider her the lead domino in their lives. I hired her because she massively changed my son's life in a matter of one phone call. He had a nutritional deficiency that she solved in moments, but then it became so much more. With her R3 program, she allowed my family to heal from emotional trauma as well. You can learn more about her on her website, TeriCochrane.com.

# Acknowledgments

THE PATH TO WRITING A BOOK COMES WITH CHALLENGES and breakthroughs. Knowing the impact that identifying and overcoming myths can have on personal fulfillment and wealth, I love giving *Killing Sacred Cows* to people to this day.

As I look over the last dozen or so years since I released that book, I see how much the world and my life have changed. The thing that has remained the same is the support I feel from my family: my wife, Carrie; our sons, Breck and Roman; my parents, Randy and Roslyn; and my siblings, Tricia and Rachelle. They have always encouraged me and given me love. Thank you.

My wife has led the charge in our spiritual life. She dedicates 10% of her day to connecting with God. Meditating. Studying. Thanks to her dedication, I have grown, I have healed. Even as we look back over the difficult moments and mistakes, she reminds me that I was doing what I thought was best for our family. She is my mirror, showing me the best of who I am and who I can be, and gently (well, mostly) reminding me when I am off track or losing sight of the highest priorities.

My path to understanding and conquering scarcity (living in abundance) was laid by a group of gifted healers.

Corey Wert, what began as a fun friendship grew into an adventure of value and play. Thanks for supporting me in releasing my worry and healing generational wounds.

Annie King, thank you for your guidance and our long therapy sessions that helped to heal my childhood pain and trauma. Your ability to listen and create a safe space were instrumental in my becoming the man I am today.

Larry Moss, little did I know how much my ability as a writer and performer was linked to feeling safe and healing my childhood wounds. Thank you.

Steven Weaver, thanks for your kind comments at the retreat in Denver and for providing me with the tools to continue on my path of love and healing.

Mike Cline, I love riffing with you, our creative projects, and your integration program—it allows me to love myself at a whole new level. Thank you.

Aydika James, in the integration process, you allowed me to see a blind spot. Now, love flows through me at a whole new level. Thank you.

Brian Yeakey, Jim Gordon, and Kelsie McSherry, thanks for helping me understand how to take responsibility for my actions, reactions and emotions. Thank you for the guidance and the lessons in how to live my vision through the ups and downs. Thank you for helping me to understand the "illusion" and how to let go and let God! You showed me that with meditation, taking responsibility, and using the LAF process (love, accept, forgive), I can navigate my way home.

Gary Kadi, we met every week for years, but it was the day you had me pull out that picture of my five-year-old self and have a conversation with my inner child to let him know that everything is and would be okay that really set my transformation in motion. Thank you.

Teri Cochrane, you are a gift. Thank you for the work you have done with my family—it has changed our lives forever. I thought it was about nutrition, but your gifts brought so much more hope, healing, and love.

Jayson Gaignard. I vowed to never give another relationship talk at an event, but then you brought me and my wife to Napa Valley. Then I joined your MMT community and learned about MDMA therapy, and the group event in Denver led me to the discovery of a whole new way to live an extraordinary life. Thank you.

Ron Zeller and Mark Kamin, almost two decades ago, I did the Landmark Forum and then hired the both of you for further support. The possibilities I was able to create after removing obstacles and living a life of integrity have been integral to my becoming a much better man, much less of an asshole, and I thank you.

I have learned so much about money, business, and marketing from brilliant and caring individuals. Those lessons have brought about so many of the ideas and philosophies contained in this book.

Norm Westervelt, you let me know that mistakes are part of the process. You have always had my back, and you turned my ideas into models that have impacted thousands of people. Thank you.

Mat Silverstein, Tom Berenthal, and Stephen Dean, before you, most of my marketing was half-baked and certainly never as effective as what you have done to reach and impact people. Thank you.

Steve Harrop, my favorite professor and racquetball partner of all time, donating $250,000 to the university for our class to invest changed how I viewed investing. Our time together shaped my career and focus. Thank you for your insight and guidance.

Les McGuire, Ray Hooper, and Michael Isom, you were my first partners, and Les, you were our philosophical leader as we spent nerdy hours dissecting ideas, analyzing financial models, and questioning everything with intellectual honesty, caring more about what was right, not who was right. Thank you for our friendship.

Darron Miller, Andrew Howell, Dale Clarke, Jeff Socha, Brett Sellers, and Moe Abdou, you make up the financial network that was the foundation for my knowledge about insurance, legal, and estate planning structures, cash flow optimization, tax strategy and everything personal finance—thank you.

Joe Polish, during a time of financial chaos, I was referred to you and within an hour and a half, your relationships made a massive difference to my bottom line. You are the consummate connector. Thank you.

I am grateful to the co-creators who dedicated their time and expertise to the creation of this book.

Corey Wert, this is the first of many projects together. I love how you can pull the best out of me, keep the reader in mind, and add your expertise to the ever-changing world of crypto. Thank you.

Marcus Hardy, it seems there is no project I do without asking you for your insight and intelligence. Thanks for going through some of these chapters to add depth and flow.

AJ Harper, well, you saved me on this one. As deadlines loomed, you swooped in to take on a role so much greater than "editor." I am a better writer because of you, and the reader will get so much more out of this book because of your skill and care. Thank you.

Dan Strutzel, this was your idea. Whether working on *New Rules to Get Rich* over a decade ago or the audiobook for *Killing Sacred Cows,* you always valued my voice, my skill set. Thank you—I will never forget the time and care you took to make this possible.

And to you, the reader: in an ever-changing world, you have the courage to face your finances—never an easy task, but worth the investment. I admire your willingness to invest in yourself, overcome myths, and conquer the game of money. Thanks for going on this journey with me.

# Notes

## Chapter Three

[1] *Click,* directed by Frank Coraci (Columbia Pictures, 2006).

[2] Stephen R. Covey, *Spiritual Roots of Human Relations* (Salt Lake City, UT: Deseret Book Co., 1998).

## Chapter Four

[3] James Allen, *As a Man Thinketh* (1903).

## Chapter Five

[4] 1 Timothy 6:10 (KJV).

## Chapter Six

[5] Janet Lowe, *Warren Buffett Speaks: Wit and Wisdom from the World's Greatest Investor* (Hoboken, NJ: Wiley, 1997).

## Chapter Seven

[6] Tony Robbins, *MONEY: Master the Game: 7 Steps to Financial Freedom* (New York, NY: Simon & Schuster, 2016).

[7] Dr. Marc Faber, *The Gloom, Boom & Doom Report,* https://www.gloomboomdoom.com, accessed March 26, 2022.

[8] Austin Rogers, "The Rich are Hoarding Cash, and So Should You," Seeking Alpha, September 25, 2019, https://seekingalpha .com/article/4293593-rich-are-hoarding-cash-and-should-you, accessed March 26, 2022.

[9] Malcolm Gladwell, "The Sure Thing," *The New Yorker,* January 10, 2010, https://www.newyorker.com/magazine/2010/01/18/the -sure-thing, accessed March 26, 2022.

[10] Marianne Williamson, *A Return to Love: Reflections on the Principles of A Course in Miracles* (New York, NY: HarperCollins, 1992).

## Chapter Eight

[11] Martha C. White, "The 1 Task Americans Can't Accomplish," *TIME,* January 7, 2015, https://time.com/3657285/task -americans-cant-do/, accessed March 26, 2022.

[12] George S. Clason, *The Richest Man in Babylon* (New York, NY: Hawthorn, 1955).

## Chapter Nine

[13] Garrett Gunderson, "The Stock Market: Where Your Money Isn't Lost, It's Transferred," *Forbes,* May 26, 2020, https://www .forbes.com/sites/garrettgunderson/2020/05/26/how-wealth-is -transferred/?sh=59bcf0365c04, accessed March 26, 2022.

## Chapter Ten

[14] Genord, Dennis, "Market Madness," BetterInvesting.org, February 4, 2021, https://www.betterinvesting.org/learn-about -investing/investor-education/investing/market-madness -short-selling-short-squeeze, accessed April 6, 2022.

[15] Denny Ceizyk, "Historical Mortgage Rates: Averages and Trends from the 1970s to 2019," ValuePenguin, updated February 25, 2022, https://www.valuepenguin.com/mortgages/historical -mortgage-rates, accessed March 26, 2022.

## Chapter Eleven

[16] Trent Hamm, "What Warren Buffett's stock market math means for your retirement," *The Christian Science Monitor,* May 6, 2013, https://www.csmonitor.com/Business/The-Simple-Dollar /2013/0506/What-Warren-Buffett-s-stock-market-math-means -for-your-retirement, accessed March 26, 2022.

[17] Garrett's YouTube channel:
https://www.youtube.com/GarrettGundersonTV.

## Chapter Thirteen

[18] BitInfoCharts.com editors, "Top 100 Richest Bitcoin Addresses and Bitcoin Distribution," BitInfoCharts.com, last updated March 26, 2022, https://bitinfocharts.com/top-100-richest -bitcoin-addresses.html), accessed February 23, 2021.